Selected Poems
2009-2021

Roz Kaveney

Published September 2021 by Team Angelica Publishing,
an imprint of Angelica Entertainments Ltd

This collection copyright © 2021 by Roz Kaveney

The right of Roz Kaveney to be identified as the author of this work has been asserted by her in accordance with the Copyright, Designs and Patents Act 1988.

All rights reserved. No part of this book may be reproduced or transmitted in any form or by any means without written permission of the publisher.

Team Angelica Publishing
51 Coningham Road
London W12 8BS

www.teamangelica.com

A CIP catalogue record for this book is available from the British Library

ISBN 978-1-9163561-7-7

In Memory of John M. Ford

Look back and count the minutes that we spent
Talking and laughing. Added up were few
Although the great good time. My brother, you
Knew quite precisely what each second meant
watched sand fall. Careless I ignore the time
Got extra when I very nearly died.
Death stole you sudden and for years we've
   cried
I cry unfair. And so I owe you rhyme
You better maker. Cannot call you back
No Orpheus stilling ThreeDog. Short of breath
to sing a navigation in through Death.
Define my talent by the power I lack.
I paint your absence rather than your face
exist dark wax-lost echo of your space.

Acknowledgments

Frank Wynne helped me make this selection.

Neil Gaiman encouraged me to use formal verse structures.

John Gordon, Lawrence Schimel and Jo Lindsay Walton have been my poetry editors and constant helpers.

Paule Searle is the love of my life.

'After Catullus 80' and 'After Catullus 63' first appeared in *Catullus*, Sad Press 2018.
'Descent' and 'Hades Speaks' first appeared in *What If What's Imagined Were All True*, Midsummer Night Press 2012.
'Awkward', 'Tangle', 'Crush', 'Cunt', 'For My Transdyke Sisters', '23', 'Requiem' and 'Stonewall' first appeared in *Dialectic of the Flesh*, Midsummer Night Press 2012.
'Endymion' first appeared on Tor.com.
'Abigail May 1st 2008' and 'Abigail May 22nd 2008' first appeared in *The Abigail Sonnets* (chapbook 2010).
'Me Too' first appeared in *Queer*, ed. Frank Wynne, Head of Zeus 2021.
'On Transness' first appeared in the *New Statesman*.

Table of Contents

POEMS ABOUT ART, SEX AND LOVE

Prayer to Apollo (March 2020) 2
The Greek Anthology 3
After Rilke's *Archaic torso of Apollo* 4
After Catullus 80 5
From *The Orpheus Sonnets*: Descent 6
From *The Orpheus Sonnets*: Hades Speaks 7
For Max Gladstone and Amal Al-Mohtar 8
Deathless 9
At the Tomb of Mike Ford 10
Bronze Poem 11
Grind 12
Logic 13
Waking 14
Turner 15
The Poet and the Poet 16
Wordless 17
Manners 18
On A Breakup 19
After Sappho 84 20
Sappho on The Lydian Wife 21
Sappho on Anactoris 22
Sappho on Age 24

Lullaby 5	25
Sappho Among the Astronomers	26
Awkward	27
Calluses	28
Tangle	29
Dance	30
Tinder	31
Potpourri	33
Quotations	34
Crush	35
After Apollinaire's *Les Attentives*	36
Aphrodite	37
Aphrodite Among the Sparrows	38
Aphrodite Pietà	39
Aphrodite Worshipped	40
Aphrodite Baroque	41
Aphrodite Burlesque	42
Aphrodite Spiteful	43
Aphrodite Envoi	44
Prologue	45
Perverse	47
Belltime	49

TRANS POEMS

23	52
Cunt	61
For My Transdyke Sisters	62

Misapprehension 63
Requiem 64
After Catullus 69
The Emperor's Nightingales 77
Stonewall – A Poem 78
My Dead Berlin Sisters 88
On Transness 89
January 1982 90
Sestina Inanna 91

POEMS ABOUT THE WORLD

Firefighters 94
The Dead Woman after Neruda 98
Winter 71 99
Waste (for CB) 100
The Poet to her Young Comrades 103
The Exiles 113

POEMS ABOUT THE DEAD

For Robert Mapplethorpe 116
For A Pregnant Friend Mourning 117
For Anna Campbell 118
Asleep (For My Mother) 119
For Iain Banks 120
Mourning Iain 121
Endymion For Neil Armstrong 122

For Louise 123
For Caroline 124
For Liz Young... 126
For Lorna.. 128
For Kathy 130
Abigail – May 1st 2008 132
Abigail – 22nd May 2008 133

NARRATIVE POEMS

Seven Sonnets from Troy: Achilles 136
        Cassandra 137
        Helen... 138
        Hecuba 139
        Briseis 140
        Penthesilea 141
        Odysseus... 142
A Scythian Princess 143
Theroigne de Mericourt... 146
A Ballad of Abuse and Revenge 149
A scribe of the house of the dead... 152
Book of the Dead 155
Me Too... 158

RECENT POEMS

Gaius Valerius' Will.. 162
The Mercy of Caesar.. 163

Birdman by Frink – Pembroke College	164
December 13th 2019	165
Abigail in Dream	166
Lilith	167
I slept so much	168
For Larry Kramer	169
The Composers	170
House in Jericho	171
Villonesque	172
For Grahame, Shepherd, Rackham and Vess	173
For Richard Dadd	174
Gambit	175
Memory of Don Giovanni	176
For Chip on his Birthday	177
Poems in a Time of Plague: Lines in a Time of Plague	178
Scripture	179
In Time of Plague	180
For Shahin Shahablou	181
After Callimachus 22	182
3 untitled poems	184-186

Poems About Art, Sex and Love

Prayer To Apollo (March 2020)

You are the God of Plague as well as Art
So spare me please I still have work to do
Some of my verse has wit and some is true
Or lies so neatly as to touch the heart
Of tough young things tall and with cat like eyes
My muses if it is not blasphemy
Compare my loves to yours. Oh pity me!
Came late back to the sonnet. A surprise
In middle age. I wish to find repose
Late style like Bach gentle hard pointilliste
Bright fragments form an arc. I have a list
Of poems still to write. And then there's prose
If I must die, indulge. Let my last verse
Infect my enemies a scabrous curse.

Selected Poems

The Greek Anthology

Short perfect verses – 'fifteen olive trees
grandfather planted.' 'I once owned a shield
shattered in battle and I had to yield'
'Your voice is soft and warming as a breeze'
'The boy I loved turned Christian, went away'
'My friend is dead, the nightingales sing still'
'Apollo cured my child when he was ill
I sing his praises.' 'Glory to the day
the tyrant fell.' We sometimes know their name,
their town perhaps. Their bones are lost to time
but something lives because they made a rhyme.
Something more durable perhaps than fame
Cold comfort in the grave, still to be read
but all that we can hope for when we're dead.

Roz Kaveney

After Rilke's *Archaic torso of Apollo*

We cannot guess its head god glaring gaze
Apple round ripe carved eyes. But yet the stare
Persists inherent in those pecs. It's there
Glows through stone muscles like the turned down
    blaze

Arclight could blind. There gentle still it burns
Warm as the sweetness of the sudden smile
That comes with loin thrust, glows continues while
The body shows self glimmers as it turns

Unwhole unshamed remaining still complete
White stone that dazzles sheen as silken skin
God like, a star that burns from deep within
Its every inch a friendly face to greet

Admonish you voice echo out of far
Far distant time. Be other than you are

Selected Poems

After Catullus 80

Most of the time your lips are ruby red
Gellius but then are sometimes flaky white
a milk moustache when you're out late at night
or if you've spent the afternoon in bed
sharing a nap. There's gossip going round
that you suck lots of dicks. And don't wipe clean,
like a memento of just where you've been
with whom. All the penises you've found
neatly tucked under togas. And at home
poor little Victor sitting all alone
stirring a stockpot with a single bone
you galivant with half the men in Rome
he strains to come and can't and wants to cry
poor chap you broke his balls and sucked them dry.

Roz Kaveney

From The Orpheus Sonnets

DESCENT

There are some very simple ways to Hell,
but none are for the living. It is hard
to leave the sunlit lands. There is a guard
not only at the Gate; the paths, as well,
are policed. He found the journey was so long
that he grew tired as death, but could not sleep
and staggered on. The way down is so steep
and each guard needed pleasing with a song
and he would have grown hoarse, but had to please
the guards with songs of innocence and love,
the harmless pleasures of the world above.
He had not thought that monsters could find peace
in such – gryphons and chimeras and weres –
could long to lay aside their savage cares

Selected Poems

From The Orpheus Sonnets

HADES SPEAKS

'I took your wife,' said Hell, 'because she died.
She died because she fled the Satyr. Chaste
and faithful to your bed. I find the taste
of faithful wives the same as those who lied
when I swallow them down. For all things fall
into my mouth. A few things I will take
– my wife for instance – just for whimsy's sake.
I am not fair or comforting at all,
I simply am. I don't insult the dead
by softening the brutal facts. Things end.
I'm there to take them, not to be their friend.
Only deluded fools are comforted.
And poets.' Orpheus smiled, strummed, sang aloud.
He'd often done well with a tougher crowd.

Roz Kaveney

For Max Gladstone and Amal Al-Mohtar

And in the forest blood flower yielding thorn
Enveloping to penetrative choke
Sap runs and floods a lubricating soak
Split sequin low-backed gown dissolves is torn
To artful origami rags. Calligraphy
Round piercing eyes along white fleshy thighs
We mete our pleasure out in quiet sighs
That speak sestinas. If you come to me
Whistle below the window of the tower
She kept me in. And I may break her trust
I'm weak like everyone who melts with lust
Dream images have ivy's stone break power
Orchid dress touches liquefy and burn
Danger kiss kill. We shudder and we yearn

Selected Poems

Deathless

All writers are imaginary friends
who whisper in my ear, throw shady looks
over my verse and prose. And move dark rooks
castle my lines with unexpected ends.
Each other's muses when the muses sleep
engaged in sly erotics of shared soul.
Die maybe done or not. The bells that toll
new measure of how reputations leap
to classic or remaindered as obscure
and then return allusions make us smile
echoes that linger. Always for a while
long life perhaps but deathless is unsure
My mortal colleagues voices in my head
may I too linger somewhere when I'm dead.

Roz Kaveney

At the tomb of Mike Ford

Strip it away. Luxuriating word
where simple clear one syllable would do.
We take the oldest themes and make them new
no myth or mask what actually occurred
the fact the date the faces and the time
yet see intensely hear and feel the pain
remembered grief experienced again
dissect a nerve and slice it into rhyme
moment the sharpest edge with which to cut
scalpel too blunt a monofilament
placed in that tender crook where life was bent
by death foreseen yet shocking. Sing it but
remember word no more than salve on ache
song makes throat sore. yet others' hearts still break

Selected Poems

Bronze Poem

You turn the winter soil. Some months ago
hawks roosted in the trees. You find a skull,
another, pelvis, thigh. White bones are dull
with mould and soil, but wash them. They will glow

almost translucent, like a shattered pearl.
Clean carefully with spirit. Let them dry.
Careful lest hungry bugs that occupy
Skull's dark recess creep out infest unfurl

a wave across your desk. And then bring paint
gold leaf a chain repurpose what was dead
as art by decoration. In your head
old pain is turned to verse. Or, so no taint

of death remains, furnace, poured wax – these may
turn shape to bronze, burn those dead bones away.

Grind

The mill is under sea. It grinds out salt.
Politics, love and death are always new.
I always have a subject – poems to do.
I sometimes think that I should call a halt

And send the Muse away. But she drops round
chocolates and flowers. And, if those fail, tears.
She left me flat for oh so many years.
Sometimes I wish she'd throw me on the ground

And call me whore because I did not wait
started to see her sisters. Ten fat books.
She doesn't moan or give them dirty looks
Just brings a sonnet every time we date.

Perhaps they're fairy gold that turns to dust
I can't believe their worth and yet I must

Logic

Logicians fall in love. They syllogize:
all lovers feel this aching in their heart
each time they see her, when they have to part.
Heartache's a symptom that they realize

means they have fallen sick, are sick with love.
Logic demands they struggle to get well,
avoid her, but avoiding her is hell.
This seems illogical, (but see above –

it is the common state that lovers share.
Logicians are all human, share the lot
of other humans, who all lose the plot
well lost for love.) Strict logic must despair.

Love turns logicians humble, sets aside
their rational, their syllogistic pride.

Waking

I wake up breathing hard, and there is sweat
there in the hollow of my back. The kiss
left me so taut. I need to take a piss
but still I throb. Of course I will forget

all details of the woman in my dream.
I know what she was like – they're all the same
too young crazy or beautiful. Their name
may vary – not the way their hair would gleam

seen on a pillow. Women who are real
quite as impossible. Love's the mistake
that makes us fools, the hard thing that we break
our sense of self upon. I want to feel

that gorgeous pain, yet most affairs I've had
balanced delight with going almost mad.

Selected Poems

Turner

We play the peacock game, scream in the night
like something's dying that was never born.
Our joy sounds like oblivion's being torn
from agony as very well it might.

For love can seem like torture as we clinch
scratch with our fingers rasp within our tongue
sweat slick come wet ejaculate among
mixed senses' information. Inch by inch

we touch each other, body soul and mind,
make witty answers to each inner touch
do things that words like fuck and screw and such
inadequate descriptions that we find

are all we can remember or can speak.
All fierce sensations leave our language weak.

The Poet and the Poet

His lyric 'A tranquillity of doves'
Her brother makes her learn when she is ten.
She's always had a vague distaste for men
Thinks him a marble spirit whom she loves.
Produces first slim volume which he'll praise
Misled by photo thinking her a boy
Whom he will flatter fuck and then destroy
Sarcastically. Thought keeps him hard for days.
Writes biting satire. Carriage on the road
She takes grand tour sees Dante's Virgil's tomb
Bribes several servants tiptoes to his room
His sleeping head a weeping leprous chode
She retches sighs one tear then slinks away
Writes him a perfect sonnet the next day.

Selected Poems

Wordless

We talk of love so much; fucks we avoid
because it's hard to find the words that speak
of how she fingers me on an antique
chaise longue, of how she grows somewhat annoyed

when I cannot quite come until she licks
the scar under my breast. Her finger still
inside me, twisting, turning; as a mill
grinds pepper at your table. My cunt kicks;

I squeal a little. Claw her back. She bites
hard on my collarbone. The stiff brocade
upholstery rashburning thighs. We raid
Petrarch or Yeats to say how we lie nights

awake in yearning, well-fucked forge our own
articulation of a squeal or moan.

Roz Kaveney

Manners

We fucked, and now I quite forget her name;
she bit my cheek, her hands upon my throat,
until I stopped her. She put on her coat
next morning, looked expectant. I didn't blame
her pout and sigh but wouldn't kiss her cheek.
I don't encourage women who persist,
with things I've asked them not to. Slap their wrist
quite gently first time. If my face goes bleak
as winter morning, you have gone too far.
I'm not unreasonable, but have my rules.
Have sex with strangers once, but not with fools
a second time. I blew him in a car
that pig. Swore any dumb thing I do once
I don't do twice, however sweet their cunts.

Selected Poems

On A Breakup

Godlike he holds her hand. She smiles. Salt tears
Headheart hurts. So you go and write a song.
They're dead. You too. The poem lasts so long
I yell at you across three thousand years.

She's smart. She doesn't shriek your name aloud
At awkward moments. Sometimes quotes your verse
He asks about you. Her replies are terse.
Smiles thinking he's not looking. Smiles are proud.

He sort of gets it. That first night he caught
Your glance, your swift departure. Treats her kind.
Comparisons are always on his mind.
You're competition still. If jealous thought

Caroms around your head like iron wheels.
You're fucking Sappho, bitch. Think how he feels.

After Sappho 84

Parting's deathsorrow. Weeping walked away
'Things worked against us, Sappho.' In her grief.
'It's not your fault.' A comfortable belief.
I found brow-stroking calming things to say.
'Child you were loved. Remember. It is known
And will be said. We managed to be kind.
Never forget the flowers we would wind
Around each other's necks or round our own
Garlands of violets. Sweet oils. And in bed
You lay and throbbed with longing. Slow as dance
In sacred grove my hand. When we'd a chance.
Often we lie and love then still as dead
Gaze broken tired into each other's eyes.'
Consoled her. Poets' words not always lies...

Selected Poems

Sappho On The Lydian Wife

She's far away. And home. She thinks of you.
Not all the time. At moments. And her smile
Lips teeth. She laughs. No sorrow of exile.
Deep distant love. So far away yet true.
You think of her as well. The sun has set.
The moon arises queen of all the night
No star her rival. Pale all-soothing light
Makes opals where fresh-fallen dew is wet
On crocus sweet electric grass. The thought
Of you of her echoes across the seas
Faster than high-bowed ships that catch the breeze
In white sails tightly rigged that snap so taut
Fast as the lightning jagged from a cloud
That does no hurt but is as thunder loud.

Roz Kaveney

Sappho On Anactoris

Some get excited when the mounted police
Trot past. The hoofbeats drive their hearts
To pulse and throb. It doesn't matter if
It's horse or rider; it all works the same
And some like squaddies, some like sailor boys
Or latex, corsetry or stocking tops.
The world's so full of lots of things to love;
Whatever does it for you. Everyone

Gets this. And she who was most beautiful
Helen, the one that we still talk about
After so many years, she had a man,
A king of men, and she walked out on him
Without a thought
And she went off to Troy
And gave no thought to any of her kids
Or to her parents. Venus took away
What little brains she had and set her off
To chase off after that dim pretty boy –
An archer who killed better men than he
From a safe distance. But she loved him so
Oh! She burned for him, like that's an excuse.
Opened hot legs and satisfied her need
And tore the world apart.

And now I think,
I have to think, of sweet Anactoris
Her swaying walk, the glimmer of her smile
And how I'd rather look at her close up

Than stand up on a balcony in furs
And watch the whole Red Army marching past
Saluting me, and killing whom I chose.

Sappho On Age

Dance. Sing. Enjoy young bodies. Let the Muse
Infuse your song the weaving of each arm
Slow dance wind saplings leaves. I once had charm
Who now have age and wisdom and white hair
Can hardly dance for stiffness in my knees
My tremble voice in waver gusts of breeze
I lift my lyre to play can't hold it there.
This is our fate. To lose what once we had
And let it go sweet bitter smiling tears
As black hair dyes to white drenched by the years
It is not any reason to be sad.
Even Tithonus faded loved by Dawn
Youth beauty's yearspan set when he was born.

Lullaby 5

I'm back. Sleep on. I'll try to make no noise
enough to wake you. As I potter round
the kitchen, making tea, the only sound
will be the kettle. I know it annoys

you to be woken – I'll put camomile
there by the bed. In case you're half-awake
and thirsty. I'll stand still just for the sake
of watching you asleep, in case you smile.

You look so young – I want to wake you, kiss
your forehead then your lips. I go away.
These are the thoughts far better had by day.
How I regret the chances that I miss

and so resent the poems that I write
when I could do far better things at night.

Roz Kaveney

Sappho Among the Astronomers

Each day we know more. Knowledge in the net
And fish and random wood. Alone she slept.
She doesn't say, so we don't know she wept.
The moon was down. The Pleiades had set.

We count the stars roll backwards in their flight.
We've known her words speak truth about the heart
Of how love ends or tears and headaches start.
We ascertain the week perhaps the night

She slept alone. Which makes it no more true
But somehow satisfies and warms the mind
With tiny certainties. I leave behind
Precise notations of my love for you.

Critics trust not her nor me and speculate
A metaphor behind each lying date.

Selected Poems

Tangle

The human heart is but a maze of meat
where muscle tangles in a gorgeous knot.
Red blood flows through it, lush and burning hot.
We wander through its paths on halting feet
whenever love begins. We feel its throb
quicken beneath us, troubling us again.
It is the one time that we welcome pain
we've felt before, we know that it will rob
our minds of dull staid, quicken every nerve,
quiver us into art. We feel the reins
that love pulls hard, our arteries and veins
harsh in our mouth. We're forced to make a swerve
where we would not have gone. Heart's such a bitch,
we know there's some new girl. We don't choose
    which.

Dance

We dance our little deaths. We press our lips
to any flesh comes near. Our hair, our sweat,
trailing like jewelled wire. Words we forget.
Our language is the grinding of our hips

against another's thighs. A smile, a glance,
a wink, a tear, a lick, our common tongue.
We'll change our partners before very long
perhaps we have no lover save the dance

it's gone past two, the moon the stars are high
light dazzles and I blink. She disappears
and I don't care, and dance. Perhaps it's years
perhaps it's moments. Darling, you and I,

dance lonely nights on this and other floors.
You'll never be my true love, nor I yours

Selected Poems

Tinder

I also know my muse will go away
to lovers, young and lithe, well-groomed and hot,
who want to fuck. Which really I do not,
nor put my naked body on display,

its creases and its sags, its whitened scars,
my gut's too near the surface and my bones
too far beneath my fat. A knee that moans
and clicks when I exert it. Sat in bars

and being charming, I can hold their eyes
upon my dancing lips and witty tongue.
They're easily distracted being young
and sometimes stroke my arms or upper thighs

which is enough. My poems, wit and charm
don't get me laid. But keep my passion warm.
That otherwise would cool. My aching heart
would stutter into age. I make my art

from broken twigs of hope, and dried out flowers
sprig left on my chaste pillow, or between
books' uncut pages. Half-thought lines I mean
to use one day, but stare at for six hours.

I stack these on my desk. Piles that grow higher
More and more useless clutter in my head,
dust, fluff and crumbled leaves, ochre and red.
These never come to life except as fire.

Roz Kaveney

But sparks will come. Affection or disdain
my muse will bring me. It all ends the same
She brings my store of words the gift of flame.
She strikes my heart to joy, or lust, or pain.

Potpourri

Your loves entwine for two years, maybe three.
She is the salt in bread, the music's bass.
And if you dreamed, it would be of her face,
But cannot sleep for love, and nor can she.

The fever drops but never goes. Look down
two storeys to a taxi, see a glove
fumbling for change and know her – it's not love
so much but she's still part of you. No noun

is quite the accurate descriptive word.
Empty a cupboard, find scrunched in a ball
a shirt that smells of her. It must be all
of five years later. What has just occurred?

Feelings deep-rooted, though they make no sense,
dried petals scent in nostrils still intense.

Roz Kaveney

Quotations

We love. But love not only as our selves.
The words we speak others have said before
who loved as much, or maybe even more.
So many books randomly piled on shelves

that teeter in the corners of my mind
all book-marked, dog-eared. I have searched them
    through
to find the perfect lines to write to you.
The fluttering archer god is wholly blind

so that he cannot read. The perfect shot
he makes pierces the centre of each heart
and it's his archery and not his art
that strikes where love should go, ignores where
    not.

Poets are never silent. It's our curse
never to love unspeaking, always in verse

Selected Poems

Crush

Hold hands a moment, for a second touch
her cheek, or pick a dead leaf from her hair.
Buy sweet red grapes for lunch, offer to share,
watch her mouth slowly crush them. It's too much

to hope for more and it is quite enough
to have these things, to have but not possess
her love, luxuriate in the distress
of stealing moments. Fragile and yet tough

wisps of desire. Accumulate your joy
fragment by fragment. Never say a word.
She's yours while she can say she never heard
a hint of what your actions speak. She'll toy

with you a month. Ten years from now she cries
awake from dreams of you, kissing her thighs.

Roz Kaveney

After Apollinaire's *Les Attentives*

It's fine. I do not use it anyway.
We all have elbows. These things sometimes break
at just a touch. Don't worry for my sake.
These things don't hurt as much as people say.

Do not be silly – it is not your fault.
Your work is touching, sweet and elegant
and its effect on me irrelevant.
I'm fine. Don't give the matter any thought.

You've an appointment and I have a brush.
Once you have gone, I'll sweep up every shard.
And glue them back together. It's not hard.
I've time, not even slightly in a rush.

Such a small thing, I'll laugh, you'll make me start
You knocked it over, but it's just my heart

Aphrodite

Dark eyes in café; half-way down the street
trousered legs strut; a soft voice on the phone.
And every certainty you think you own
will be destroyed. You do not have to meet

the woman or the man glimpsed in a bar.
Their face illuminated by your gaze
a second, then you think of them for days
Lust takes you. All the things you think you are

Faithful or queer or straight. She takes the net
in which her husband trapped her once, and throws
it over us. Don't fight her, for she knows
the secrets of your heart. She's love, and yet

she's hot as blood and harsh as cruelty
and wayward as the white foam of the sea

Roz Kaveney

Aphrodite Among the Sparrows

She loves her sparrows, watches them all day.
It's her idea of resting. Feeds them grain.
Smiles as they cluster round her while the rain
is falling and she keeps them dry. Their play

their fluttering so often turns to rut.
When sparrows mount, they chirrup squeak and trill
in small hot ecstasies that rise until
they satiate. Sometimes she cracks a nut

crooking her smallest finger – feeds the meat
to favourite birds that come at her command
and peck it from the hollow of her hand.
She quivers from the light weight of their feet

As sensual as they but far more strong.
They trust her, eat, continue with their song.

Selected Poems

Aphrodite Pietà

It did not matter who had sent the boar.
There was no vengeance in her. Only tears
fall where a tentative red bud appears
drops of his blood turned floral. Nothing more

not even wailing. Silence. In her lap
he lay. Fierce tusks had torn the youth. A shred
of gut nearby at random. He was dead
before she heard him scream. And yet the sap

still rises in the cedars, and the corn
that died as seed is growing in the fields.
She knows as goddess the next harvest's yields
will fill the granaries. He'll be reborn

The streams of Lebanon in springtime flood
bring fields fertile red soil. Adonis' blood

Aphrodite Worshipped

She often walks among us. In high heels
or sometimes flats, because her feet get sore.
Sometimes we feel a momentary awe
rush of affection lust – the kind that steals
up on us unaware until we sweat
a little, breathe quite hard. She's walking by,
just catch her sideways glance, her lightning eye
is on you for a second. You'll forget
you saw her, but her glory's aftershine
illuminates the next girl that you date.
Sometimes you please the goddess, feel her weight
next to you in the night. Touch the divine
when it is offered and you have the luck
to be the random one she picks to fuck.

Aphrodite Baroque

You take it from the top. And then repeat
with longer trills. Strings make a noise like storm –
a cold high flute. Compared to it, you're warm
who otherwise would be harsh steel on feet.
Your hair is high, pin-curled and powdered white.
Your cheeks are dotted red, a doll's sweet face.
Your voice so loud it fills this velvet space
and exits echoing. It thrills the night
the night where lovers lie. And in your box
watching yourself, you sit. Behind your fan
you weep and laugh in turn. A rataplan
shocks in the orchestra. Amid stage rocks
you mourn lost love, hit notes of glory pain.
You sing and watch, feel truly and yet feign.

Aphrodite Burlesque

Somewhere out in the light, the goddess' face
most of what stabs my eyes with light. My tears
burn down my cheeks. We've been like this for years
or so it seems. The details of this place
are vague. A vast yet maze-confusing hall
where velvet tatters hang. Are those her dress?
Parts of her skin? I hardly want to guess
what she'll take off. The sultry drawl
with which she summoned me to watch her dance
let no refusal, but was full of threat
of painful things that have not happened yet.
Each time she calls me here, I take the chance.
To glimpse in mirrors fragments of desire
that chill to stone, heat beyond flame or fire

Aphrodite Spiteful

Sometimes she wrecks things just because she can.
A goddess sometimes has to show her power.
You draw that card – and lightning strikes a tower
that tumbles. If you thought you had a plan
it's over. Oscar crazy for the boy
who wrecked him. Or Francesca with the book
that sent her off to Hell with one shy look
at her brother-in-law. And then there's Troy
talking of fallen towers. She caused all that
ten years of war, young heroes in their graves
wives and grandmothers killed or sold as slaves.
She wanted to be fairest, like some brat
wants sweets and throws a tantrum in the street
then sat back smug and bloodstained in her seat.

Roz Kaveney

Aphrodite Envoi

She's with you for a while, will always fade.
She's spread so thin. Her legs are spread as well
for far more lovers than she'll ever tell.
A goddess has her secrets. You'll get laid

a while and think you love her, are loved back.
It's sort of true, and sort of really not.
Sex is her work – well, that and being hot.
Come home one day – and she's begun to pack.

Her stuff's not in the wardrobe. In her case
are all her toys. She's hung up your spare key.
She pecks your cheek, a bit maternally.
Then she is gone, with heartache in her place.

Yet it's a sort of mellow, gentle pain.
Love never wholly leaves. Will come again.

Selected Poems

Prologue

A sense of painted eyes and dark red hair
Across a room; perhaps we met and spoke.
I sipped my tea, not sure why I was here,
noticed as you do some friend of friend
you may not meet again. I sipped and left
I wanted to get home and write some verse.

Her face sometimes appeared, when, writing verse
I thought of beauty. Or perhaps her hair
the precise shade I needed. I was left
with her in mind. Lifted my phone and spoke.
Talked easy as to any older friend.
A week or two, and then she moved

to other cities. I stayed scribbling here
sestinas, sonnets, other sorts of verse
She read them sometimes, Facebook was the friend
shared them with her. Showed pictures of her hair
distracting me from verse. We never spoke
wrote once or twice. We'd met and then she left

Her image was the trace that she had left
You listen to my verse, and you will hear
whispers and traces. But I never spoke
nor thought of her, except that in my verse
red dress, sly smile, her finger twining hair
flash past, no more than any other friend

Roz Kaveney

My verses speak so much of friends. This friend
I hardly knew. There's not much story left
I travelled, rang her, met for lunch. Her hair
was as remembered. There's no tale to hear.
Held hands a little. And I knew my verse
would change, and she'd be all the words I spoke

A little while. It was of her I spoke
Said Aphrodite, muse, but always friend
teasing a hint of love in every verse
Knowing I would not see her soon, I left.
She was so far away, my life was here.
We kissed just once. My finger touched her hair.

These words I spoke the best of what is left
Chose friendship even though there's aching here
turned into verse, but ah! Her russet hair.

Selected Poems

Perverse

There was one time, wax hot tight on her skin
cracking a little as she squirmed beneath
my sharpened thumbnail, breathing through her
 teeth
a little harshly. Pausing I sipped gin

the lemon slices bright, the bottle blue
as sky; she feigned a struggle with her chains.
I let her sip then pulled it back. The pains
we take with lover's needs. I took her shoe

red patent leather used its heel to score
small puckers on her thigh. And heard her moan
and sometimes felt more truly on my own
with her than when alone, could not ignore

that she'd forget and cry in ecstasy
on other's names that she loved more than me.

And yet she came to me, knocked twice, slipped in
using the key I gave her. Love has been

less kind to me than being used I fear,
when unrequited. Better to face facts
perform perverse and quite delighful acts
than sit hope lust weep know my sweet my dear

would never love me. Better be her whore
her backdoor lover and at least get laid.

Told her to kneel before me. She obeyed.
Because she did not love me. Passion's claw

sharp in my flesh. No scream, a poker face.
Cruel ingenious hands, coldness of heart.
Act well the torturer's not the lover's part.
Play hunter, be the chaste prey of the chase

Belltime

Belltime black spark. Joints passed on iron stair
Red smear kiss quick in mirror broken glass
Love sudden random hand deep on your arse
Splashed stale smoke lager sweat in short blonde
    hair

Mandala painted leather. Broken zips
Open to breast dark armpit sudden heft
Hand clutches. Know who made love when they left
Who sweated lonely, memory on lips

Which did not follow through. Until next week.
Two years we cycled through and lust around
Went love hate glory pain. The things we found
And then the music. Memory's a tweak

Pinches old scars. We danced there for a while
Now gone to weep the tears that make us smile

Trans Poems

23

We all know how it works; we've read the books.
There are no whisperings across the years,
Advising or consoling. Good job too.
Change one thing and the web of self is torn
The world is sad enough without such tears
You've read the books; we all know how it works.

You can't read this. It doesn't change a thing.
It's just a way of talking to oneself,
And not one's young self. There is no way back
But there's no real thing without pretence.
Pretence of which all memory is one.
It doesn't change the thing that you can't read.

You're twenty-three. There's books you haven't read
Not written yet, gadgets you've not switched on,
Not yet invented. Not to patronize,
That is the hardest part. To keep in mind
The things you know, and didn't get from books
The books you haven't read. You're twenty-three.

You're still a boy. You didn't mean to be
By now. You're scared of taking the wrong path,
Of never moving, and of being poor,
Of being killed. You need to take wrong paths
You have to die to move. Right now, although
You didn't mean to be, you're still a boy.

Selected Poems

The plan was yours. You were the architect.
Who built a self that you could not yet see
From hope and fear. The stuff you didn't know
You made up; the things that you let go
Built paths in time, lit bridges through the dark
You were the architect; the plan was yours.

That year they put your friends behind the wire
You spent your lunch-breaks leaning on a wall
Your friends would cluster and you'd tell them tales
Or sing or anything to keep them true
The whole yard at their backs, that they'd ignore
To stay your friends, put there behind the wire.

The yard behind you, your side of the wall
Echoed with fights and games, and no-one sang.
They'd pull you from the wire to stand in goal
Or burn your wrist with gripping, twisting hands.
Your friends would wait and call and drift away
Leaving the wall, and you off in the yard.

Your father worried over how you walked
And would not let you act in the school play
For fear that they would cast you as a girl
And make him speak aloud the thought he feared
And start to lose the boy he'd dreamed you were
And how you walked worried your father's dreams

The Cubs, the Scouts, long walks and throwing balls
He'd hoped that you could whistle, or see jays

Roz Kaveney

That he'd point out. Still, you could manage knots
Tell tales of ghosts, cook pastry over fires
And snared a rabbit. Not a waste of time
Long walks with him, thrown balls, the Cubs, the Scouts...

Your father's scouting days were innocent.
He did not know what boys do in the woods
Or how you built a dam and stood on it
Ten foot of water held back by your hand
To make the older boys leave you alone,
In innocence, like Father's Scouting days.

Helping to make bread god, in robes and lace
Passing the wine and oil, tinkling the bells
Knowing the words and sounding them so fast
The other servers wagered on your speed
Worries of flesh like cobwebs torn aside
Spirit in robes and lace, to make bread God

The scurf on old men's tongues, the reek of wine
Air stale with mothballs, caskets full of silks
And gold brocade that snagged a fingernail
Driven away the flesh will still return
Nagging till spirit blows away like foam
The reek of wine, the scurf on old men's tongues

Your virtue irony in a friend's eye
The more you knelt, walked Stations, told your beads
Peter would snicker. He knew who you were
The confidences of long walks to school

Selected Poems

The thoughts that hang where reticence betrays
A friend's sarcastic eye watched you be good.

The name came first. You knew that it was yours.
You wrote that novel – God, and it was bad –
You let it go, and held the one true thing
The yellow notebook told. The girl was you.
The Rosalind you'd made up from yourself
You knew that she was you. The name came first

You read the books and they were full of fear.
Hugh Selby's Georgette had a rotten life.
John Rechy's Destiny was cute but strange.
'I want what I want' was not how you felt.
Anthony Storr said they and you were mad.
And you were full of fear from reading books.

The books taught many things apart from fear.
They taught you where to look. The bars. The street.
The street was kind to you. You were so young
And no-one hurt you. Ava, Sylvia –
Both helped because you were their younger self,
Afraid. Like books, they taught you many things.

Her house smelled of washed dogs and boiled cheap
    meat.
Sylvia lived there and you went to stay.
She taught you makeup, how to be a whore,
But that you shouldn't have the life she had,
That you could have a different woman's life
That didn't smell. And where there were no dogs.

The bars were fun, though. Though you could not see.
Your glasses did not go with eyelashes.
Men said that you were pretty and you drank
The praise and drink they brought you, so you'd stroke
Their cocks up backstreets, or in darkened cars
Where they could not be seen. The bars were fun.

Those were weekends. You had to go to school
A little stoned, with eyebrows that were plucked,
And no-one noticed, or perhaps they did.
The boys had pretty much all handled you
They'd called it bullying, but it was sex.
You had to go to school. There were weekends…

You hope and pray. You never learn despair.
Your classmates dangled you above the street
And did not break or drop you. In the dark
You whispered prayers to silent apathy.
All night, and still smiled in the morning light.
You never learned despair. You pray and hope.

You made those choices that you had to make –
The street, or Oxford. What you chose was hard,
The choice that gave more choice, the waiting choice,
To lie, and be, and not yet own the name,
And live in books and dreams and memories.
You had to make the choices that you made.

*

Selected Poems

There is a lush life there behind your eyes
A life you've stolen out of comic books
From Chandler thrillers and from musicals
Where you can twirl or pull a twenty-two
And kiss or blast those who are in your way
Behind your eyes, the life you lead is lush.

Music has taught you how to live in times
Where frenzy alternates with intellect
Sweet flute is answered by dark trumpet call
And chaos turns to pattern. So you hope
For order out of tension and dismay –
To beat in time, the way that music taught.

Music and dreams. You sleep away the years
And hope to dream and not to choose.
Let friends harangue you, let them choose your name
Until your sadness nearly breakd your brain
You weep, and choose. And wake out of the hurt
From years of sleep, and music, and of dream.

Nobody died yet. That changed everything.
Your heart's unbroken and you don't know loss.
You'll learn from time which rips and leaves a tear,
Where there was love. Love is the only thing
That goes away and yet is always there.
Everything changes, though, when someone dies.

You find new bars, and streets that are less kind.
You can't pay back. Sylvia is not there.
You pay along, and help some younger friends.

Roz Kaveney

Others you cannot help – drugs and despair
Police rape, bad boys, and worse decisions, so
On streets even less kind, you find new bars.

The day you change, like any other day
Is sunny or is rainy. You get up
And put your new clothes on, and brush your hair
And put that on as well. Your breasts are sore –
They still have stitches. And you drink your tea
Like any other day, the day you change.

The men you'll love are elegant and tall
Arrogant, English. There'll be Alastair,
Magic the only love he does not cheat,
That chokes him in the end. They are all bad
For you, and never will be yours.
The elegant tall men whom you will love.

You nearly die. Parts of you rot away.
You burst an artery, and lie in bed
Putting on weight from drugs that never work
Translating poetry to check your mind's
Not turned to porridge. You learn to survive.
Parts of you rot away. You nearly die.

Men walk away. It's women who remain.
Women who fuck you near insanity
Women who bite and ask you for the whip

Selected Poems

Or flash their arse when you bring breakfast tea
Or spoon against you in the dark of night
Women remain. It's men who walk away.

You're on their list. There are so many lists.
You're stroppy, queer, demonically possessed,
A woman made not born, made by yourself
Born of yourself. You're not supposed to choose
And yet you chose, were born in blood and pain.
It's hard to list whose many lists you're on.

They don't kill you. And they don't kill your friends.
Shadows are dangerous for what they hide.
Hatred in boots, and knives that cut like words
The words and knives that cut the years in half
The time before, and time that had been cut.
Cuts that don't kill your friends, and don't kill you.

You have to trust life. When trust is betrayed
Build it again, look where you were the flaw
That broke the crystal. Look into the glass
And see your traitor face, your face betrayed
And know you are the crystal, and the flaw,
Whose trust's betrayed.. To live, you have to trust.

The woman you will be. She's quite the thing.
Not quite as pretty as you hoped to stay
Much liked, a bit admired, and wrote some books
Had heartbreak, broke some hearts, and stood up tall
For all that you believed in. You'd like her.
She's quite the thing, the woman you will be.

Roz Kaveney

Horribly vain, as well, and greedy too.
Smug, slattern, feckless and a nasty tongue,
A gossip who plays games, but plays to lose
Out of neurosis, never seeing through
The projects she begins. These are her faults,
She's greedy too, horribly vain as well.

Just to be fair, you have to see both sides.
You may think that the good outweighs the rest
You might not. Of the faults, all I can say
Is that you had to be there; of the rest
That it was damned hard work to manage it.
You have to see both sides, just to be fair.

You're twenty-three. There's stuff you need to know.
Learning to let things go is one of them.
Let go to keep the moment fresh and fair
Things are so fragile and so transient
You hold them crystalled: let them fly away.
There's stuff you don't know yet. You're twenty-
    three.

Cunt

The surgeons left me with a patchwork cunt,
stitch-marks and scars, and smooth skin flayed from
    thigh.
I bled. I oozed. With speculums, I'd try
to burn new keloids off. I'd grope and hunt

for small hard bits I'd missed. That now are smooth.
Things levelled out. You'd never know the sore
torn places that were there. For an old whore
it's sweet and neat and innocent as truth.

I paid in blood and pus. Here's what I got.
Not some mere hole, but tenderness. A maze
of flesh love's fingers have explored for days
and found its spring, gushing and furnace hot.

I dared not hope. Yet my reward was this –
to hang in ecstasy on sweet girl kiss.

Roz Kaveney

For My Transdyke Sisters

Perhaps excessive neatness, or a scar
that spirals round the hood. You press your lips
against it, and she squirms up with her hips
and you lose track a moment. We are

all so prone to giggles of astonished joy
that what was hard won was a total gain.
Fingers force inner scars, a little pain
but worth it. She is wet. Let's not be coy.

Some of us love our sisters. On a date
saves time, we can avoid the big reveal.
They told us we were sick. Here's how we heal,
here's how those storms of self-contempt abate.

We bite and lick and groan in sweet surprise,
then check our lip gloss in each other's eyes.

Misapprehension

Apparently I smell. Or so they say.
Those women who are always on their guard
against my kind. They walk round, sniffing hard.
The scent might get lost on a rainy day.

It's life or death. Imagine their disgrace
if perfume or a smoking cigarette
confuse them. And maybe, worse thing yet
scent-lost, they see a smile upon my face

and smile right back. It happens, and I flirt.
Some people say I have a deal of charm
What if they ran a finger up my arm?
And someone saw? Their name dragged in the dirt.

Their sisters unforgiving of such slips.
Pus and hibiscus on three finger-tips.

Roz Kaveney

Requiem

1. FREE ME

Choose
fold into darkness
self-woven shroud.
Melt away and mould.
Burst into sudden light
fragile, moist, true.
Choose
never to swim again or know the tides
breathe harsh bright air
burning dried salt-flaked gills
throat married to new songs
walk, knife-feet stab each step.
Choose
not to be dark veins or light.
Chiselled wings burst free:
the folds of robe
carved, fixed in flight,
single trumpet note
piercing.
Choose
new
kitten-blind
foal-totter,
moth-flutter
boy-strut
girl-smile
angel-song.

Dance.
Choose
to forge yourself
from ice and steel
from marble and from gut
from blood and bone.
True name, true face, true song, true dance
innocence, danger and delight.
Choose
The life you would repeat a thousand times
However short, however long.
Your dance.
Cut short.

2. DAY OF TEARS

Some of them
walked streets I've walked
under grey clouds
had friends I have
listened to songs I love
or drank in bars where I
would drink (if I still drank)
Some of them
knew other skies that have no clouds
sang other songs
and never drank at all.
Still,
my sisters, my brothers, our kin, our kind
singers, dancers

flesh and bone
made choices that I made,
and died for it,
lived lives we walk
and died for it,
and so I mourn for them.
We mourn for them
Here, now.
Duwanna, Andrea and all the rest.
Destiny
cut short

3. WRATH

Walls curled
Around walls.
Spirals, grid, broken.
Door leads in darkness
to other doors
or to blank walls
that curl
around.
Blood reek,
blood spatter,
old stains
layer on layer.
Scrap of gut.
Shard of bone.
Blood, shit and fresh dung.
They put you in the rooms

Selected Poems

The dark rooms curled around
The dark rooms open to the sky
Where the monster got you
where the monster ate you.
Dumb savage twisted
Whose horns scrape on close walls
whose hooves slide in the blood
Whose tail, whose prick
juts, swishes, swings
Menace and rage.
You, tribute, offering
Sent to dark rooms
Walking dark streets.
Heavy breath steam behind you
Hoof-clip, horn-scrape.
If not you
Someone who
Matters
Mother, brother, lover, child.
Yet you are all those things?
Not in the way that counts
And not to them
The ordinary decent folk
Who'd never kill, but close their eyes
And do not watch.
It's closer now.
Time that you turn
Fight, kiss, pray, scream
Or maybe leap the horns
Choose.
Cut short

4. ETERNAL LIGHT

Joy is a choice whose absence is despair.
We learn to walk, to dance, to fly.
Freed into light
free into brilliant air.
The beast learns nothing. Its own misery
traps it among curled walls
in darkened streets
where it strikes out
with hooves and horns at joy
And it would steal joy if it could
It never can.
The blood upon its floor
The blood in which it slips
Its victims'
Its own tears as well
Despair's blood tears.
We weep our dead
In different tears
that mourn and yet are joy
bright as the chisel-strokes that gave us wings
piercing as trumpet note.
They loved and danced
for moments of that joy
in brilliant air
and if they were cut short,
dance still
bright
in tear-stained memory

Selected Poems

After Catullus 63

Attis hurries. Runs barefoot,
takes a fast boat to Asia,
runs again.
Mad with Her love so that he feels no pain.
He loves.
Comes to Her woods and groves.
Then starts to cut
cut with the flint that cut
feet.
Cuts deep and fast.
The blood begins to flow.
She plucks the last
Bits of her former flesh
Out by the chords
No.
Takes off their weight
loses that weight.
So
And slash
No words for what she feels
new made at her own hand
blood gushes on the trampled earth
at this new birth
of who she is,
of what he was,
of who she will be,
what he cannot be.
Her hand
Suddenly delicate white hand

Roz Kaveney

Seizes the tambourine
The little tintinabulinking
tambourine
the drums, the drums as white, the calfskin drums,
    drums of Her sacrifice
cut from the bull-calf.
Stretched
stretched
drum beaten by the white hand
the light hand
fierce.
She sings soprano, sopranino, mezzo mezzo to the
    band
of her new friends, her sisters of the cut
who beat the drums
and wave the tambourines
and dance upon the ground the bloody ground
the sound, the echo sound, the piercing sound
of Goddess rite.

Step forward, step back, one two three
Left, forward, right, back, one two three,
Stamp skip step, stamp skip step,
stamp skip and kick.
Step, stamp and kick.
We are the girls, kick,
girls of the cut, step
Cows for our Lady, stamp.
To her woods we go, step.
Far far from home, kick,
exiles for ever, left,

Selected Poems

birds of a feather, back.
Sisters of cutting, kick.
Follow my lead, stamp.
Cast aside Love, kick
Watch Goddess laugh, left.
Hurry together, kick.
Dance to her house, right
Deep in the woods, stamp.

Where there are flutes, kick,
where Maenads shake it, back,
wild curly locks, left.
Cymbals clash, crancrancrancran
Drums beat, ratatata
Howl howl howl howl
Honour the goddess
One two and three, stamp
one two and three, kick.

Attis dances, Attis sings.
Attis new girled.
Howls. Howls. Ulualalalu
Drum ratata, cymbal ratat.
Up to the mountains
wild in the trance.
Out of breath out of mind fast stamping chorus
bleeding bleeding white
Drum ratatat
Cows moomoo ullalalu new
to the yoke
the goddess' yoke.

Roz Kaveney

The goddess house.
Where they drop
drop
sleep
starved
emptied
and frenzy
done.

Glare of the morning. Sky burned clear.
Waking sun.
Line of light across the harsh rocks,
the dry land, the scrub land, the merciless sea.
Wild horses of the sun
chase shadows of the night.
And Attis
wakes.
Wakes in the arms
of the mother goddess of all gods.
Calm of frenzy
Awake
Fresh from cutting, fresh from dancing,
voice clear.
Looks out across the sea
and sings homesick regret.
Aria.
O patria mea
quanto mi costa
Distress
you made me you undo me
mother and mistress,

Selected Poems

I flee you
as slaves flee.
Up to the high hills
the hills are so cold
the wild beasts shiver
among them am I
snuggling in dens.
Oh country,
mother and mistress.
Are you here, am I there?
You have high hills
where trees shake in winds.
This is my home
driven by frenzy
far from good people kind people gentle folk
High harsh hills.
I am not in the forum and I am not in the gym
I am not in the marketplace or running round the
    track
I am no more that person and will never more be him
I've left my home forever and I'm never coming back
Regret regret regret. Ullalulalu
What does she look like
what do I?
Woman – stamp
Boy – stamp
Husband – stamp
Groom – stamp
Girlfriend – stamp.
Wife – stamp
Eunuch – stamp.

Roz Kaveney

Maenad – stampstampstamp.

I was so cool
they loved me in school
the best in the gym,
they asked me to tea,
they turned on the fans,
they brought me flowers, so many flowers.
And that's all gone, ullalalu
up in the high hills.
Cut.
Like a slave
slave to the goddess.
Wild hair, and bleeding, cut.
Ullalalu
Among the pines
with boars and deer.
What have I done?
Ullalalu.
Mercy, mother, mercy. Hear my woe, ullalalu

The goddess heard.
Her lions roared
the long-maned lions who pull her chariot,
sweet chariot.
And said.
ROAR
ROAR
Drive Her Mad
With your Roar.
Whip her to frenzy with your lashing tails

that lash, that smash, that slash.
ROAR
let her feel claw.
So she's mad. Mad.
Then let her run mad fingers through your mane
your hair your lovely hair
your strong neck.

Goddess takes the yoke from off their necks
The lions howl, and prowl and yowl
There is a crackle in the undergrowth
it's lions seeking prey, tracking prey,
prey that runs from the hill
crosses the stream.
Running water running water
Make me safe.
Tracking Attis as she prays
kneels in the sand
looks across the sea.
White sand under delicate white knees.
And
They
Pounce,
Roar
In her Ear.
Drive her quite mad
Slave forever. Slave to the goddess.

Goddess, hear my plea
Goddess, stay away
Her but not me.

Attis but not me.
Ullalalu
Cut

Selected Poems

The Emperor's Nightingales

'Your feathers were torn out of someone's side
left blood behind, and were then dipped in gold.
They're dead things, can't protect you from the cold,
and you're dead too,' the angry songbirds cried.
'Your music's dead – a string of cog-wheels whir
inside you, and pluck strings. You can't replace
real song, of which there'll never be a trace
in you. The soulless blind artificer
who thought with you to steal our songbirds' soul
has failed. You're a pathetic stupid thing
too dead to know that you can't even sing.
Just parts of music. While we are the whole.'
And while the palace garden harshly rang
with nightingale complaints, the toy bird sang

Stonewall - A Poem

1.

When there is a riot
is like
when there is a crisis
in a lot of lives.
It is when a hinge creaks,
when a hinge swings,
and things change.

The place
where there is a riot
where there is a crisis
That wasn't important
till it was important.
Important for what happened there.

Stonewall
Was just a bar
Where gay men
and some dykes
went to drink
Or to get laid.
It wasn't a bar
You went to
if you were
Too poor, too queer, too young, too brown.
It was a bar
Down the street.

Selected Poems

One night
it was the place
where things changed.

2.

You have to remember
you have to imagine
you have to feel

how things were,
back in the day.

Some nights you went to a bar
And your life changed
Not for the better.

The police would come in
Because no one had paid them
Or just 'cause they could.
And the police dragged you out

You stood in night court
Or lay in a cell
with drunks, hoods and thieves
who knew you were queer
so worse than they were
and no-one heard you scream.

The press took your name
And printed your name

And that changed your life.

You lost
Your job
Your home
The marriage where you hid,
Your childen and your future and your hope.

And people went to bars
For all the reasons people go to bars
To drink, or to get laid.
And sometimes their lives changed.

That night
At the Stonewall bar
lives changed
and some for the better.

3.

We don't know all their names
The people in the bar
when the police went in
And then things changed.

So make them up.

Harold was there
After the symphony,
Or after La Boheme –
He'd have to check.

Selected Poems

He keeps his diaries still.
You don't call him Harry,
Or Harriet,
He's Harold. Still.

He went there
Because he wanted a drink
and wanted a fuck
and Judy had died
and he wanted a friend.

Arnie was there
He worked construction,
He wasn't queer –
He told himself.
He wanted a blow job
And not to have to pay.

And Harold spoke to Arnie
And Arnie had a beer
And Harold had a white wine
And then the police were there.

And Harold relaxed
And was sad about Judy
And dreaming of the man who got away
And Arnie thought well
I'm fucked
If this gets out.
On the construction site.
So Harold shouted fuck off pigs

And Arnie shoved a cop
And somebody hit Harold in the head
And Arnie said don't hit my friend
And then it all kicked off.

Or, it wasn't quite like that.
It was Betty
Who taught school
Out in the suburbs
And was talking to Dean
Who had an Elvis quiff
And could fix your bike better than any man.
And a cop told Betty he could fuck her better
And ran his fingers up and down her spine
And Dean said, fuck off pig
And then it all kicked off.

Or it was Baby Val
There for her birthday
She was just eighteen.
The first time she'd been out
Wholly in drag – and she just cried and cried
The pigs had ruined her birthday.
So she cried
And then it all kicked off.

4.

And so the police, they dragged
Harold and Dean
And Betty and Arnie and the rest

Selected Poems

Out of the bar and out into the street.

And then it all kicked off.

And they held Baby Val
Inside for questioning
And someone screamed
The pigs are beating Val in the back room
And then it all kicked off

The riot was the bar
And
The riot was the street.
The street where people lived
The street where people walked
Too young, too queer, too poor, too brown.

Looking for handouts
Or daddies for the night
Or cheap street drugs
In drag and out of it.

The people with nothing to lose.

I know their names
Because they are my kind

Marsha P. Johnson – Present
Allyson Allante – Present
Tammy Novak – Present
Zazu Nova – Present

Roz Kaveney

Birdy Riveira – Present
Stormé DeLarverie – Present
Miss Major – Present
Holly Woodlawn – Present
Sylvia Rivera – Present – Probably
In spirit anyway
So print the legend –
Sylvia was there
And maybe threw
The bottlesmash we heard around the world

And all the rest
Drag queens and street queens and hair fairies and gender illusionists and Warhol superstars
Street Transvestite Action Radicals
– but that was later
– still they were all there

In jeans that looked like you could peel them off
like fruit skin
like peach skin
like grape skin
In eyeliner and eyelashes and paint
So thick it didn't crack
so thick it didn't run
tear gas made no impression on that slap.
And showgirl stockings

And their hair fluffed up.
Hurling dustbins
in high heels

Selected Poems

screaming screaming screaming queens
We are the stonewall girls
We wear our hair in curls
We wear no underwear
We braid our pubic hair

And they were all so young
Sylvia was seventeen
Sweet seventeen
Allysson was fourteen
Parents threw trans kids away
So young back then
Marsha was twenty-five
The oldest lady on the street

And it kicked off
And Tammy ran away
Hid in Joe Tish's flat
But she'd been there

And it kicked off
And Holly got there late
In time to throw a brick
But she was there

They were the stonewall girls
They wore their hair in curls

They are my sisters, so I sing of them
Like Homer did dead heroes
And they're dead, the most of them.

Sylvia's liver went
When she was fifty
Marsha – she was found
face down and floating
in the Hudson.

Allyson's still here, married again,
and Holly, just about.
Sometimes trans folk make old bones.

The stonewall girls
Their hair in curls

Don't no-one ever say they were not there.

5.

This much we know
That night everything changed
And they were there
All of them, they were there.

The ones I know because they are my kind
The ones I know because I made them up

They changed their lives
They changed all of our lives

The hinge creaked
When the door opened
The police came out of the bar

Into the street
And we came
Out of the closet
Into the street
Out of the closet
into the street.
Out of the closet
into the street.

Roz Kaveney

My Dead Berlin Sisters

Poured drinks in bars perhaps or sold a dance
to drunk-dare men or sang in small reviews
or whored of course. If not the life they'd choose
in perfect worlds, at least it was a chance

to be themselves if just for those few years
jazz cocaine glamour Charleston shimmer gown
and permits that would let you strut through town
quite legal. And they paid for it in tears

the cute red bob shaved down until it bled
the quarry and the wire the random shot
you got to be a girl they say you're not
the club the boot the bullet to the head.

We may not last. So dance fuck every night
you can. And if they come for you, scratch, bite.

Selected Poems

On Transness

I knew when I was four. Girls were my team.
Boys were the other side. Not as distress.
Something I knew. Not yearning for the dress
my best friend wore at parties. In a dream
we danced and flew. Flesh silk in every twirl
Feet stars. And no one followed, no one led.
For many years they told me she was dead.
She found me when she looked for me as girl.
Mourning was lead. But these things were all true.
Things I knew not to say. Silence my friend
I feared that they would catch me in the end
Nailed to unchanging skin. Be just like you.
Which I was not. Nor am. I represent
this chosen model of embodiment.
Mingle my elements alchemic gold
Quicksilver flows even when sick or old.
Some things I choose. And some things are my fate.
Stories a web of both. Spun spider time.
Sparkle by chance, by choice smear waste dust grime.
Early I knew, transitioned slightly late.
And paid the ferrygirl my toll in full
the blessing of pus blood months weak in pain
if free would chose it over all again.
We all have weight to shoulder or to pull.
Perhaps you'll hear me if I say it clear.
You live a body set and formed and grown
I change my flesh and mind and not alone.
We come among you dancing, year by year.

Roz Kaveney

January 1982

Took agony my lover deeply thrust
Between my thighs an ache pierce pelvis deep
Trapped to my core in gorgeous ravished sleep
Lodged inextricable white iron lust.

No second inquisition will I fear
Racked by my choosing pear-stretched until torn
This was the labour out of which I'm born
Laugh pant sweat fever soak withòut a tear.

Flay patch and soak in salt exquisite pain
New-knitting nerves that thrill delirium
Is death like this? Wake nights I think I come
So close then fade to doze then wake again.

Taken and paid for in delighted choice
Bargain of screams that scarred and cracked my
    voice.

Selected Poems

Sestina Inanna

They hold me at the border of my soul
The guards strip me of bracelets, dress, skin, charm
I stand there naked yet my name is truth
No harm can touch me when I speak it loud
I am the only goddess that I know
Descend to Hell and find myself in pain

There's grace in knowing all the guards of pain
that cut me in my face, my limbs, my soul
There is a grace we only naked know
stripped down past ugliness we find the charm
naked in a white gown I scream aloud
dead, drugged, bled out in ulcers I find truth

The guards of Hell have branded me with truth
they cut my tongue and whipped me into pain
My gurgling screams are truth spoken aloud
Read on my skin the words that form my soul
they strapped me into hell, I learned the charm
that freed me. Words are all the truth we know

The border is the torment that we know
And crossing it our only word of truth
Stripped down past skin past bone we find our charm
and scream aloud the only spells we know
carved from our body we remake our soul
from severed broken throat we sing aloud

Roz Kaveney

Broken and mended words we sing aloud
sweet painsongs that from torment we now know
guards Hell and torment formed out of our soul
bones broken mended source of our new truth
the glory goddess made out of our pain
skinned ghastly lovely shining smile of charm

In age we learn truth is the only charm
true naked words we learn to speak aloud
we learned stripped out of language into pain
in Hell we learn the language we now know
imprisoned bittersweetness is our truth
the regrown language of the chastened soul

Speak goddess, pain the border into charm
Inanna is my soul who sings aloud
the Hell I know that carved me into truth

Poems About the World

Roz Kaveney

Firefighters

You wake. For seconds try to stay asleep
Bladder is full, legs tensed. You feel around
others are waking stretching. Feet hit ground
Screaming alarms, each mobile phone went beep

over and over. 'Where's the bloody shout?'
'North Kensington, that's miles.' 'It must be bad
to bring us all that way.' At once you've had
a sense the world was turning inside out

with you caught in its folds. And then outside,
dressed, all equipment checked and neat and clean
you have to get it right, or it will mean
your death or other's. And the one who died

May not have been the one who was to blame.
You drive and twenty sirens break the night
And in the distance black and sick and bright
the reason why you'd woken. Tower of flame.

Twenty four floors, how did it catch so fast?
You do the sums. So many people there
the middle of the night. You draw in air
slow as the breath that might soon be your last.

Let it out slowly. Look round at your team,
especially your partner who now draws
a finger across her throat. There is a pause
then the slow treacle action of bad dream.

Selected Poems

You couldn't park at first, the street was packed
with other engines, cars, and then the smell
burnt plastic and the dead. A body fell
twenty floors down, her bones teeth skull spine
    cracked

Snap broken matches. 'Are you ready? Go.'
Into the dark you stumble onto stairs
Outside the noise of screaming swearing prayers
inside things breaking crumping. How you know

it's bad is when there's nothing you can touch
even with gloves, when everything is hot
under your booted feet. You sweat a lot
no air but what you bring, which isn't much.

Your partner's with you, keeping up the pace
slow steady step by step and taking care
almost anonymous in all you wear
You know her well and cannot see her face.

And do not have to. Under mask and grime
the same expression wonder, fear and pain
how did it catch so fast. You climb again
Each step is spending breath and lives and time.

You cannot see floor numbers in the dark
and have to keep a count inside your head.
There's someone on a landing. Check, they're dead.
A crackle and your intercoms both bark

Roz Kaveney

'Somebody screaming twenty-second floor'
You think you're on eighteen. You're almost there
you check your gauge. You're almost out of air.
Then something slams. Smoke gushes through a door

Man woman. No one else. They think they heard
Someone on higher floors. You stop and think
Look at your oxygen, Smoke makes you blink
Downstairs, they sent you to the twenty-third

That's not an option. These won't make it down
without your help. She's pale, begins to faint.
Your partner catches her. The smoke's a taint
even in your clean air. Shake head and frown

And call it in. And then start to descend
Man leans on you. Your partner carries her.
They'd not have made it. Always you prefer
lives you can save. There's some things you can't
    mend

Your partner's a new mother. If she dies
Another orphan. You've made the tough call
He overbalances. Catch him – both fall
to the next landing, crash. You bruise both thighs

But nothing's broken. He's still walking too
limping a bit. Your air is running low
but share it. Lights ahead. That's how you know
He's almost safe. You see he lost a shoe

Selected Poems

His foot is burned a little. Point it out
to medics when you hand him over. Hug
a second. They inject him with some drug
a sedative. Her too. They take them out

You follow. And your mate. Into fresh air
Well, fresher. Now you recognize your thirst.
The second bottle goes down like the first
not touching sides. The third gets almost there.

You rest a moment. Well, at least you try
there's people left to save, dying in pain
You get an air tank, and go up again.
You save the ones you can. And do not die.

Roz Kaveney

The Dead Woman after Neruda

My love, I shall live on when you are gone.
I hate to say it. Out there in your night
I would be silent. And there is the fight
Blacks beaten men in prison. When the sun

shines a last victory that's not mine but ours
I must still live – forgive me from your grave
For living still when rising like a wave.
Sun warms blind face. If dumb still sing dark hours.

Your death falls tatter red and yellow leaves
rain soak fire burn cold freeze. My broken feet
Stagger from death where you and I would meet.
You wanted a strong unbroken one that grieves

walks on. The people march. I am among
them writing singing marching am their song.

Selected Poems

Winter 71

Sit on the bus with her then wait outside
reading two novels. She is very pale.
Taxi back to the flat. A quiet wail
suppressed. A box of tissues when she cried.
Bled in the night. It stopped. I changed her bed
and washed the sheets. The endless cups of tea
with too much sugar. Tried to talk to me
again about what happened. How he said
that he'd be careful. Wasn't. Should she phone?
We didn't think so. Saw him in the street.
wondered if I'd be rude if we should meet.
She did not have to face it on her own.
I helped her. And it doesn't matter when.
Her sister now. I'd do it still. Again.

Roz Kaveney

Waste (for CB)

Dead buggered boy breath – even if not true
a rumour's potent threat, gossip goes round
ties wrists. There is no air beneath the ground
where buried bodies lie. To me and you

word comes as fear. What might they do to us?
Restraint unknown. Broken ungiven word
story of death that may not have occurred.
Tale forged forgotten without noise or fuss,

each sin a chain of air that slowly binds
like wicked brothers tied by deed and blood.
They did the bad thing that they might do good
scent of sweet rot infuses changes minds.

Whispered betrayal poisons with a hiss
constricts our acts in numb paralysis
Libation blood soaks ground. Rare precious dirt
its clot crumbs speak to wrap the world in noise.
Red drip spoil mark stain rich neck's diamond poise.
Mock her – your speaking shares you in the hurt

done to the woman with the severed hand.
Talk to your friend with crystals that you stole
out of her earth. And back then she was whole.
Man came with knife. It was just as he planned.

Deplore their wars. And think your pale skin white
Not innocence, but ash or leprosy

Selected Poems

Do it to Julia and not to me.
Death tick we hear in watches of the night

that stump drip. And we lie to get some sleep.
We did not do it. Blood earth mud we weep.

From the sky, falling, screaming. Dying. Fire
that day. And ever since, blood-soaked excuse
almost illegible. No win, all lose
stakes of revenge chips piling ever higher.

Eyes watching, everywhere is on a screen
real turned to game. He checks in each day
presses a button when he's told to play
no talk or dream of fire that he's seen.

He aimed. Fire fell. And so that one man dies
name on a list, it flies small vicious bird
bears fire. Might not be there, we only heard.
A wedding, village or a child fries.

Fire is our fear and guilt, our fate, our shame.
We live from fire. Fire kills in our shared name.

We walked on cod shoals, but we ate them all.
The rains don't come and then the rice crop fails.
One voice another stilled, the song of whales.
Embankments crumble, profit towers fall

Roz Kaveney

Gold church where money's Holiest of Writ
And dying with no toys the only sin
Tantalus thirst, it rises to our chin.
Undrinkable from oil, gas, soot and shit.

Lungs full we drown although our throat is dry
Black water's dead; it has nor leaves no air
Even the Styx is dry. We need no fare
Bright burning bluer than your eye last sky

At dessicating lies we choose to wink
Crucible chars our throat melts gold to drink.

What look like dunes are piled white dust of bones
what glints is buttons, fillings from our teeth,
the bullets used to kill us, and beneath
the rotting plastic of our mobile phones.

Elsewhere of course, just white. It looks like snow
for they had nothing. And now lost their lives.
One coughs, eight billion die, no one survives
for long. And through our roads wild flowers grow.

Silence at last. Before, a rushing crowd
running and dying. Trample and fall down
and trampled. Come to rivers, run in, drown,
last song, last poem. Is our screams. Are loud.

Deafen through steel walls the last rich man,
scraping last caviar from his last can.

Selected Poems

The Poet to her Young Comrades

1.

You will not all live through this. Death will take
you unexpectedly. Shot in a crowd
rushing police lines. And if I am allowed
by circumstance and age – my heart will break –

I'll write a poem for each death. My friend
was special and is gone. That's what we say
in every elegy. And then I may
incite some sort of violence at the end.

I'll still write sonnets, and that little turn
in the last couplet will break people's hearts
read at your funeral. And so it starts
the peoples' angry rage. I'll see them burn

your killers. Yet know, with a guilty sigh,
It was my verses sent you out to die.

2.

I have forgiven several of my friends
betrayals so bad they will break your heart
as they did mine. Quite soon, departures start
among you – lovers, comrades. Never ends

this agony of watching things go wrong
in times of trouble. One will turn to drink
and slowly die. Another start to think
small compromises best, self-sold belong

among the worst there is. And yet his face
still has the smile you loved, as with a moan
reluctantly he sends the robot drone
that kills us each in turn. I hope for grace

to curse, love, understand such traitors still.
Stare coldly in their eyes, then shoot to kill.

3.

These are the worst of times that I have known.
I'd like to say they'll pass, yet fear to lie.
It's probable that some of you will die
before all this is done. Will die alone

in exile or in prison, slowly starve
die from diseases we know how to cure
be left to die from them because too poor.
Worse yet, know while you live your every breath

is stolen from those poorer. Make them count
each angry moment, live write fuck and dance.
You cannot choose your time. So take each chance
to live. Remember me. Give good account

of who I was. And make the bastards pay
who kill our world, our lives, our brief lost day.

4.

To fight the tyrants we give up our name
become the rebel only. Spend each night
on different sofas. No life except the fight
we fade dissolve. And so become the same

Anonymous as roses. Change our voice
to electronic buzz. A pastel vest
padded or binding hides or fakes a breast
The world has left us very little choice

Masked save for eyes and mouth, witness and speak
And have no fear of death, because no life.
The policeman's gun, the state assassin's knife
All power theirs. Our options are so weak

Save to refuse to serve, refuse to cry,
refuse to live and dying, never die.

5.

We quarrel, often. And of course it's true
and rarely trivial. We'll get it right
although it means we sit up half the night
in rooms, on Twitter. Such a shame that you

will not accept you're wrong. As obstinate
as Trotsky, though no ice pick to the head
occurs. Because we do not want you dead
just very sorry, dialectic's weight

heavy upon your chest. Then you confess
quite insincerely, but we do not care.
What once was solid melted into air.
The question's time-expired, well more or less.

Just mentioned briefly in some final bitch
when fascists shoot us all in some deep ditch.

6.

How do you love in hiding? On the run?
When every hour is precious, how begin
to talk of love? When there's a war to win,
your deepest intimate a well-cleaned gun

For hours you practice taking it apart
putting it back together. You can't learn
lovers like that; you've not the time to burn
learning the way to stimulate each part

take them to bits, then snap them into place.
Guns only ever talk to those they kill;
you have a need for conversation still,
or heart grows steel. It's there in your cold face

Worst tyrants sometimes from best comrades made.
So risk it, fall in love, at least get laid.

7.

It's you instruct me. All I do is tell
you what I've learned. Perhaps I summarize.
You need to know what I've seen through your eyes
that we can use. My generation fell

Comfort seduced us. This time they'll use fear
to break you into bits, devour you whole.
Each of us has a kapo in their soul
to do their work. And some will disappear

At random, just to keep you on your toes.
I'm old and toothless. I will write things down
you've told me, hold your words here, when you
    drown.
They are not quite as smart as they suppose

Some of us whom they thought they'd bought and
    sold
find something left of rebel when we're old.

8.

We might well lose. Our enemies are smart.
They have the guns and money. And the power.

Do not assume that this is not their hour
to gloat, stamp on each face and break each heart

that cares and weeping sees the world decay
music and kindness. They won't understand
why victory seems to crumble in their hand.
We'll die in pain. And quite soon so will they,

Our only consolation that we told them so
Cold comfort of correct analysis
inadequately argued. Synthesis
Perhaps the last sad true thing that they'll know.

Death's dialectic. Ashes of our brains
Mingle with theirs. Hot winds sweep empty plains.

9.

So many fights we can't afford to lose
so fight we must. With blood upon our hands
perhaps. Important each one understands
it is the fight, but not the blood, we choose.

Fight that's our dialectic changed to will
we do not fight to win, perhaps to save
some fragments of what Money would enslave.
Freedom and love. I do not want to kill

Reluctance has a price we might not pay
but others. Pox and ignorance and ash.

Selected Poems

Unending brutal tyranny of cash.
Perhaps it does not matter what I say.

Blood answers me and sneers. Intoxicates
Kills innocents, yet throws down nightmare states.

10.

It's almost sexual, that sort of rush.
A meeting listens to you. Feel their hearts
your hand upon their strings. That's how it starts.
You get addicted to that breathy hush

in meetings when you speak. Like good cocaine
it makes you briefly sharper than you are.
Words race round corners as you'd drive a car
hand brutal on the wheel. And it's your brain

whose tyres you burn, but also it's a cause.
That's more important than soliloquys,
or disagreement sobbing on its knees.
It is the people's struggle, and not yours

Beware of leading. Easy to enjoy
the ride. The revolution's not your toy.

11.

You do the things that only you can do,
be useful, kind in unexpected ways

to sisters and to comrades. When malaise
creeps over you, accept it's like the flu

you are allowed to spend a few days sick
a few days off your game. Recovery
is sometimes slow, never obligatory.
You learn doubt's shape. It fits, a sudden click,

part of analysis, that's never done
always in progress. Brick on brick gets placed.
Each momentary problem that you've faced
part of the process. Always try to shun

the simple lying versions leaders sell
that silence stories only you can tell.

12.

You'll probably outlive me. Unless shot.
If things get bad, as very well they might
And we're arrested on some foggy night
I will not last in Dartmoor. Feet will rot

joints creak I'll catch the flu or fall asleep
and not wake up. This happens when you're old.
Bad food, some brutal guard, or just the cold.
They'll put me in a grave twelve inches deep.

And burn my poems. Keep them in your heart
where they belong. Admonitory advice

to learn, digest, remember. Once or twice
use them to teach. Yours is the harder part

suffer for years kept going by the hope
of seeing your tormentors choke on rope.

13.

It may well be that they will kill us all.
A thousand bullets in a thousand brains
would solve most of their problems. What remains
of any opposition will soon fall

to broken hearts and age. Yet, tense, at night
they'll brood on murders missed. Fear that we'll rise
somehow from death. Their lies will glamorise
us to their shiny children. What we write

somehow survives, however much they burn.
Regrows like bindweed, underneath the ground
Your essays and my sonnets will be found
on barrows, shelves and websites. No return

for you or me, my dears. We're dead and gone.
Their children praise us. Freedom's just begun.

14.

Or maybe not. Perhaps we lose. The worst
not knowing, but suspecting, as we die,

these fools have killed the world. And don't know
    why.
Desperate people rise up, and the first

shot down as we were, and the next. Paid thugs
kill sisters brothers hoping they'll not starve
yet do. In south and north great icebergs calve.
Floods rise. Crops fall to blight or rot or bugs.

Last child falls to last sleep pus in her eyes.
The last birds charcoal on last burning trees
Art knowledge love just ash on smoke-filled breeze
charred dust with husks of roaches, lice and flies.

Those curses true we screamed with our last breath
Dying rich men will fuck the world to death.

Selected Poems

The Exiles

Their bread tastes bitter. And how steep their stairs.
My knees are old. May I come back to Rome?
I'll write an epic. All those postcards home
With coded love. He finally despairs,

Lies in the sweat sheet bed and gulps the pills
Letters of transit never quite arrive.
Of those last poems very few survive.
The landlord threw away. Broke lungs on hills.

Ice pick smashed skull. Once they blew up her car
to show they could. Bribe border guard. Again
Forged papers ink runs standing in the rain.
He writes home's food light garden. It's too far.

Old sick and hated. If they want me dead
Come find me here asleep in my own bed.

Poems About the Dead

Roz Kaveney

For Robert Mapplethorpe

When we cry for the dead, it is ourselves
We cry for. Images in black and white
Flicker through tears. Sharp bone pale in the night
Across the years. His memory on shelves

Refrigerated so that it might last
So that the silver printing cannot fade.
Sweat stank on leather each time he got laid
Penis like tender orchid curve carved mast

He celebrated fame and flower and fuck
Worked as a demon with dark angel hair
Love sex chose models and they are all there
Ambition art cash chequerboarded luck.

Faustfisted bargain passion love and fame
Boiled monkey skull will always call its claim

For A Pregnant Friend Mourning

White from no sun no blood the wasted hand
lifted from bed and helped to one last touch.
It is so little and it is so much,
We think we hope that he could understand

feeling new life as his began to ebb
on its last tide. Could feel the belly swell
two pulses. There are moments we can't sell
or buy. Our lives are twitches on the web

that ties in love and friendship. You to me,
you to this dying man I'll never meet.
Love is a dance of many running feet
relaying passing batons. And the sea

takes him away and takes us all in time
and all that's left is songs and love and rhyme.

For Anna Campbell

The wind across the water blows her hair
Sun bleached across her forehead and her eyes
gaze at us quite amused. When the peoples rise
she goes to help them. Breathe the desert air.

Eat lentils bread dark honey. Sip mint tea.
Sleep tired no bed on earth baked stone and dust.
Sisters knife rifle boots are what she'll trust
while anyone is slave she is not free

so every war is hers. The empires lie
say they will always win. Their boot in face.
She watches dies. Her liberty's a place
to kill bleed hold stand firm salute defy.
Her brown eyes firm smile asks for nothing more
than someone else's everybody's war.

Asleep (For My Mother)

Her breathing on that last day soft and slow
A little troubled moment then to calm
And back to sleep. I reached and stroked her arm.
Was that we both were there something she'd know

Or had that passed? Eyes flicked from side to side
Hearing two voices. Did she recognize
That I was there? She looks up and then tries
To wake a little. On the train I cried.

And I had said goodbye and so had Jane.
It was we did not know last of her days
There is the last word that a person says
They tire. Drugs sleep and death the end of pain.

Last glimpse her sleeping face closed eyes her skin
Against the bedding pale white paper thin.

Roz Kaveney

For Iain Banks

A poet cannot lie. Must tell the fact
that people go, in pain, and cannot stay.
Last month, last week, last hour of final day.
He took my hand. And my voice might have
    cracked

but his did not. A sort of madcap grace
he had. We used to think it was the drink.
He'd laugh, be serious, dance on the brink
of parapets. No mask behind his face.

He wrote, once, of a gentle alien spy
observing, liking. Someday going back.
That wasn't him. He has no chance to pack
some souvenirs. He won't leave, he will die.

Cheeks slightly gaunt, his shy sardonic smile
haunts, like his rich sad sweet rococo style.

Mourning Iain

Sky porridge grey. No sun. Along the quay
a skittish wind bites cold face, aching head.
loose pages blow like gulls, cannot be read
because not written. There's a sort of glee

in so much sadness. It's the rictus grin
grief's ache puts on each face, that and the cold.
We mourn him not as we'd have mourned him old
complete and done. We mourn the might-have-been

One handshake more, one joke, or one last book,
We'd squeeze them out of him, like drops of blood
if we could keep him, selfishly, we would.
Remember how he smiled pained, one last look

Farewell as he worked expertly his last room.
One crow road feather for hearse horse's plume.

Roz Kaveney

Endymion For Neil Armstrong

In her white silent place, the hangings dust,
grey pebbles stretching to the edge of black
so far away. The goddess feels a lack
somewhere elsewhere, an ache deep as her crust

and weeps dry tears. The gentleman is gone
the first who ever called. His feet were light
as he danced on her. Went into the night
quite soon, his calling and his mission done

yet still his marks remain. Footfalls and flag.
The others she forgets. He was the first
to slake her ages long and lonely thirst
for suitors. Now she feels the years drag

as they did not before he came to call.
Our grief compared to hers weighs naught at all.

Selected Poems

For Louise

We are the thoughts that we can recollect
Persist and pulse the beat of melting clocks
Chase as it disappears bright tail of fox
Strutted as owned the park. Time vulture pecked

Her from herself. Her beauty nail sharp wit
Lasted until it did not when the glass
No more showed her her self. And these things pass
Clouds bubbles memories. I'd like to hit

Time in the face so hard. All summer long
She played the same damn record Tapestry
Weaves mighty real taste of Earl Grey tea
Poured endlessly. And still the same old song.

She is not here. Was not before her death.
Yet in my mind laugh smile and husky breath.

Roz Kaveney

For Caroline

Not my muse, clearly. Caroline was drunk
Vodka and malice were her nightly food
And yet her work could be so bloody good –
a style taut and electric as the bones
that made her lovely even in decay
sodden old age lit once or twice a day
by what had been, what canvases still show
beauty laid over crone for time to carve
passion for joy that too much joy would starve
a killing fun, that breaks as you enjoy
each moment costing wisdom how to live
in happiness, and in return will give
genius for pain, and talent to dissect.
She was so cruel with a sort of truth
served anger envy, never joy or youth.
Broke hearts, shattered her own elegantly
bright fragments shone as tears around her neck
jewels of style to decorate the wreck
that years and vodka made her. Husbands saw
her cat, or sharp-toothed siren or as line
of perfect harmony. Hard to divine
what she'd have been with will to choose her fate
rather than live for men, and booze, with art
only a thing she did and never part
of who she was. She taught me, at her feet
sozzled on her divan, the art to sneer
pleasure of self-contempt, seductive fear
of never getting life or art quite right
One of my goads, the voices in my head

not good enough, lazy, and underbred
so fuck you, lady, also thanks a pile.
For booze and bitch, for lessoning me hard
in fucking up and getting some things right
how beauty, talent, grace can still be marred
by dark self-will and still give sullen light.
Not muse, she was my Fury for a while.

Roz Kaveney

For Liz Young

Her eyes less made up than calligraphised
Her beauty intellect burning through skin
a calvinist of literature not sin
She hated what I wrote, would hate this now.
Said poems should be passion shouted loud
her rule was that no rules should be allowed
and she convinced me with her diatribes
not least because she cared enough to scream
at me I should be wild enough to dream
my own dreams, not the steps in a career
She was not wrong – with nothing left to lose
I did the right thing when the time to choose
Arrived. Her acid tongue burned art away
left me with life to work on getting right
told me my charm and wit were rust and blight
I had to live my life in earnest, care
about integrity. She disappears
out of my life for several crucial years.
Was the Rimbaud of critics, fingers burned
down to the bone with booze and sex and punk
avant-garde book-selling and smuggling junk
We meet again with all our dramas done
Middle-aged women writing sharp reviews
Both in poor health but she had better shoes.
Lined up in rows under the mantlepiece
above the gas fire where she huddled warm
scribbling in notebooks. She still hated form
and praised wild chaos though her life had ebbed

and loved the irony that her disease
was caught in childhood. Cat across her knees
Dying in two mirrored brocaded rooms
postcards and masks and dolls and ornaments
around her. Dressed in shawls and cerements
And sipping tea, and sniffing opiates

You were one of my saints. You feared your mind
would go before your liver. Tried to find
some hope and had none. Left before the end
You chose to make the drug your last good friend
whether to die, or throw life in the air
for chance to take or not. Did not despair
so much as wake up and decide one day
to pack your bags and see what death would say.

Roz Kaveney

For Lorna

A balcony, and twilight, and the noise
of night's cicadas. My glass full of wine
and hers of vodka. There's a ball of twine
upon the table, and a plate of cheese.
Some olives and some bread. Some sort of cake
red berries in it. Something she would bake
sometimes and sometimes buy it from the store.
We'd talk for hours, or sit and read. She'd drink
slowly and steadily. Make notes, then think.
You saw a smile growing behind her eyes
of something understood, something acquired
that was not thought of, not even desired
until she had it whole within her grasp.
Eyes that had mischief in them, sometimes rage,
then she'd look down, and turn her notebook page
and work on something else. Until she'd cough
those wrenching noises tearing from her core.
She'd look embarrassed. Worried that she'd bore
her friends and guests by being mortal sick.
A woman in a hurry, who found time
for friendship, food and joy, thought it a crime
to waste the years that she had left. She'd laugh
that throaty phlegmy laugh deep in her chest.
And plan your time. Being her friend and guest
meant you walked Florence for her. Climbed the hill
behind the house in the last hour of night
to see the city laid out grey and bright
washed clean by dawn. Walk paths through long wet
    grass

and tell her over breakfast. Find some trat
and eat bollito misto there and chat
in halting Tuscan with the owner. Walk
back through Oltrarno. Tell her over tea
the sights and tastes and sounds. And she'd tell me
the things half-seen half-tasted that I'd missed
but she remembered from her walking days.
I wish some image, some remembered phrase
stuck from our talks, but words just evanesce.

A gossip, a tale-teller and a flirt,
who'd sit dishing French Theory with the dirt
on every poet, every novelist.
Pause, think, go back and mock the ones she'd missed.
But not for malice. Was the finest judge
because it was for Art she held a grudge
and never for herself. Those who let down
their own best work, she'd mock around the town
then over drinks would tell them what to do.
And all her caustic remedies were true.
She wrote her own great book just at her end
My teacher and my sister and my friend.

Roz Kaveney

For Kathy

Each of her stories was a labyrinth
You might find truth out, or poetic lies
she thought as true and often were. Her eyes
as honest both ways and her smile as sharp
her teeth just catching flesh behind a lip
she stuck out, daring you to catch a slip.
Mostly you didn't, only got a part
of any story, contexts drifting past
in tatters, till exhausted, at the last,
you thought she'd told you years of a short life
– more years by far than she had told you of,
more lives – as daughter, scholar, dancer, love
of men and women, skilled at holding back
in love, as truth. Her art was never coy
but told less than it said – hard to enjoy
if you thought its flayed skin and bloody bones
not staged, and bitter, brilliant mime of pain
cavorting madly and yet coldly sane.
She talked, and did not lie, of how tattoos
were ecstasy by inches, yet took pills
to numb the pain, yet for each pain she kills
Others, imagined, felt in sympathy,
affected, and yet bruising through soft skin
working their way through flesh and further in
and crumbling harsh into her skeleton
into the marrow. Pain avoided was a loan
she fully paid, each image of crushed bone
mirrored a truth she kept behind her eyes.
To boys was straight, to girls a total dyke

Selected Poems

In-between truths weakness she could not like
whose world was absolute and never shades.
She could not walk to death without fierce cry
of Murder! Wildness not so much a lie
as one last drama torn from life in claims
that she'd been poisoned. Cruel to the man
who loved her, kinder to the art whose span
drew to its end in classical repose.
Restraint almost and delicacy too
from love and life, drama and art withdrew
to quiet sorrow, and calm gentle death.

Ghost! if you came to me one night in dreams
boasted how nothing stops you – that's no lie –
some find and love your books. Also, you wore
tight jeans, primrose with leopard spots, and more –
clothes that your last girl says she saw you buy
Last time you spoke to me was truth, it seems.

Abigail – May 1st 2008

They broke her door and found her two days dead,
Perhaps a few hours less. Her hairless head
Lolled on two pillows, upright in the chair
where she was dozing, layer upon layer

of rugs to keep her warm. Her blood ran thin
from drugs and chemo. She had never been
So tired. Her heart had stuttered, guttered, died.
A can of beer, an ashtray by her side

Yeats book-marked with her bus pass; spine-cracked
    Joyce
her dog-eared favourite books. I miss her voice
drunkenly phoning late; how she would stab
her cigarette to point a joke, and grab

at life, a life she knew is no good friend
to bitter, lovely women in the end.

Selected Poems

Abigail – 22nd May 2008

The head burns slow; the heart burns slower still.
The thin burn quickly while fat people fill
ovens with sudden wildfire, char the bricks.
And what's left afterwards is just a mix

of fine white dust, misshapen bits of bone,
screws from your crowns, perhaps. And all you own
sits in a cousin's attic, or a skip
out in the street. A memory of your lip

quivering on a nipple, or a speech
you gave once, lasts. But very shortly each
of those who loved or hated you will go
through the same process. This is what we know

without a question. Everything will pass
cities and mountains, songbirds and sweet grass.

Narrative Poems

Roz Kaveney

Seven Sonnets from Troy

For CN

In memory Christopher Logue

ACHILLES

The third time round the walls, Achilles thought
of his dead boyfriend whom he'd quite forgot
though only one day dead, untouched by rot,
in all the hours that he and Hector fought

evenly matched in beauty strength and skill.
Fights have no idle moments, but time slows
as thought does not. And so the thought arose
he'd like to fuck this man he had to kill.

And spear-thrust sword-slash were like lover's play
until that final thrust, that final breath,
the death of heroes, and the little death
the hero feels who does not die today.

He dragged the corpse until it had no face
but knew he'd see it in Patroclus' place.

CASSANDRA

She was so proud and clever, but the curse
took cleverness away. Just keeping track
of when she was, and always going back
over the major bits. She would rehearse

her rape, her death, the horse, her father's death,
over and over. Get the order right
tick off each day's events each wakeful night
each stomach upset, sneeze, shortness of breath

Knowing that she would know it rabbit fur
no help before they told her. Carved in stone
each second, and she'd witness them alone
except for all the other times of her

that saw them unbelieving. Her sole friend
the death that put recursions to an end.

HELEN

She was the perfect weight to assay gold,
length's measure and the note at perfect pitch.
And if she felt compelled to play the bitch
at once to have hot loins and mind that's cold

to toy with nations and a lover's heart,
how else be free, how else to have a life
save slash her cheeks to tatters with a knife?
Gazed at, not heard. If she would sometimes start

to talk of her desire, they heard her voice
only as music stroking them to heat.
Paris massaged the small bones of her feet
and did not touch her flesh. He was her choice

because he saw her, not the face or hair.
Some myths say she was never really there.

HECUBA

To be a queen was glory. Drank it all
sweet wine and rich, then bitter, then its lees
and dregs. Her husband Priam on his knees,
white hair turned red with blood. She saw Troy fall.

She saw her children die or raped or slaves.
She saw too much and then went barking mad
and cursed the Greeks. There's sorrow beyond sad
and howls beyond lament, madness that raves

beyond unreason. Did not change her skin
to dog as some men said but leashed so tight
her grieving thoughts that snarling through the night
they hunted all of those who slew her kin.

Few Greek kings lived long. Fewer kings died well.
Their Trojan victims mocked their fates from hell.

Roz Kaveney

BRISEIS

She was no traitor, but she liked the boy
and then his love, her master. Saw the way
they touched each other's hair, and day by day
grew comfortable there, so near to Troy,

so far their tent from war, although each night
she scrubbed blood from his tunic, bathed the sweat
of war from him. His captive, slave or pet,
unclear. In bed, both men would hold her tight

Sometimes, but kissed each other. Men came, took
her off to Agamemnon. It assuaged
her grief that while her lord Achilles raged
no Trojans died. He came for her. His look

melted her and she helped him wash his friend.
As she would wash him too before the end.

Selected Poems

PENTHISILEA

It was not their war, but it was a chance
to fight a war and show the race of men
what they need showing time and time again
that Amazons can pace that blood-pulsed dance

better than any. They came to the war
tall slim fair killers, trained for sixteen years.
Archers and foot and twenty charioteers
who did not care what they were fighting for.

Greek poets claim Penthisilea died
Achilles killed her, kissed her dying face
made her a warning – women keep your place.
She never fought him, and the poets lied.

Swept the field clean for one short brutal day
killed all who fought them, laughed and rode away.

ODYSSEUS

The goddess came and saved him once again.
We had him and his son, knives at their balls,
down, sweating. Then a voice like struck brass calls
out of the air. Our king had killed our men

taken one generation to the wars
and killed their sons for hanging round his wife.
I wish I had been quicker with my knife.
He hanged my daughters, said that they were whores.

The island dies. No one to guide a plough
sow seeds, make pots, bake bread. We will grow old
and starve. He has not even brought home gold,
just death. That's all that Ithaca grows now.

Athena guards him. Otherwise our king
would be dead meat, not one of whom men sing.

Selected Poems

A Scythian Princess

She was a princess
and they found her gold
among her bones
tiaras, three of them,
round her grave-weathered skull.
Horses galloping where once her hair
waved endless like the grass
the grass her world.
Their hoofbeats never stir
her empty eyes. She slept beneath the grass
and mice, the small mice of the grass
crept in
and ate her fingers to the bone
and then the bone
She slept so sound the mice
could scurry into her, and never wake.

She was so tired.
Her sixty-seventh year
Their grand-sires' fathers
brought and dried the reeds
that wove her cradle
and saw her walk
a proud sad child
up to her father's chair
of reeds and gold
and then sit herself down.
Her feet just reached
the floor

Roz Kaveney

She healed the goats' pox
and she brought the corn
Talked to the Hellenes
charmed your warts away
and drew her knife across her lover's throat
one line of blood to bring the rain
one line of blood to curse an enemy
his throat torn out
his guts torn out
thrown to the waiting birds
he trifled with her
fingered the sacred girl who brewed the milk
the girl she could not and she would not kill.
Princesses both on grass without a queen.

The girl died. Lightning marked her death
and marked her grave. And then her brothers died
arrowed in ambush. Tears that would bring rain
no weeping for the dead.
She cut her robes, knife-cut her flesh
blood spattered on their grave
curse spattered those who killed them
who died soon, drunk, poxed, starveling and insane

and she rode on. Each horse she rode
greyed, stumbled. Meat for stew
its bones for flutes and needles.
she greyed and did not fall
her skin so soft
where butter eased the lines.
Her eyes as sharp as rain

as wind her mind. Her words
the quiet thunder in their minds

She slept one day and just forgot to breathe
it seemed to them. They stood and did not move
for fear of chiding. Sent their youngest child
to touch the lips, and listen for the breath
and nothing but the wind. They danced for her
slow mourning waves like grass in wind and rain
painted her skin in ochre, henna, woad
with sigils of her life and many deeds.
They built a shelter round her, burned the hemp
and breathed its madness, fathered many sons
all to be sons of her long barren life.
Sold horses to the Hellenes for the gold
horses that were their brothers on the grass
and hammered horses. Wound them round her head
and raised an earthwork higher than the grass
and laid her in it. And then rode away.

Theroigne de Mericourt

Somebody told them of Theroigne de Mericourt
all those tough women,
who pushed market stalls
all the way through the streets to the poor quarters
up from the quays
where they sold day-old fish
carts that brought turnips
– you cut out the rot –
calling on bakers who put out stale bread for you
that you could soak
in water and milk
and make it fresh again
eat it with chicken heads,
pig feet and marrow bones
turnip bread fish-bone broth
what the poor eat and not like the food that she ate
luxury diet for Theroigne de Mericourt.

Someone came down from the club of the Jacobins
showed them engravings of her with her tits out
drinking champagne, eating something called caviar
came to their clubhouse, and bowed to them courteous
like a good citizen, not an aristocrat
where they sat comfortable drinking from tankards
smoking their pipes on a warm autumn evening
resting their feet from the sores of their wooden shoes
with stays unlaced, them as wore them, for comfort

petticoats open, legs open to cooling air
just for the pleasure and not the depravity
nothing like lecherous Theroigne de Mericourt

She was no citizen though she pretended
she had a head that was full of ideas
no-one should have – that were all about women
Women should vote, women should speechify
women read poetry, storybooks too,
make fancy love like that bitch-whore the Queen
not push their stalls, through the cold before dawn
not make the broth that keeps children alive
not lie in bed with your husband asleep
staying awake to give him a thick ear
if he comes at you to make a new child.
She was all fancy, in sleeves that were slashed
big floppy hats that nobody would wear –
that's how you'll know she is Theroigne de
    Mericourt.

Somebody told them she needed a lesson
told them her friend had just gone to the scaffold
friend called Olympie and what kind of name was
    that?
Probably slept with her, wrapped her legs round her
all those aristos are perverts and sluts.
She though was clever and was not found guilty.
Full of her lawyer's tricks, treason in petticoats
needed a lesson in what decent citizens
thought of her nonsense, and here's where you find
    her

sipping her coffee among decent citizens
even though she's evil Theroigne de Mericourt

Battered her senseless with broth-spoons and
    wooden shoes
shattered her hand with the wheel of a cart
kicked in her face, how dare she be pretty
left her in street dust and pissed on her there.

That was the end of fair Theroigne de Mericourt
left there all damaged her looks quite destroyed
hardly could speak and forgot all her poetry,
never could wear fancy clothing again
lay in a cell, in her filth, and grew old there
sometimes they pushed her out into the yard
swilled water over her, washed her to cleanliness
not that they care for her, just for the stink of her
sometimes exhibited Theroigne de Mericourt
that is what happens to women above themselves
women believing they think like their better halves
Even the street sluts know better than that,
even the worst of them, blood on their petticoats
kicked the ideas out of Theroigne de Mericourt
face full of old scars and brain full of rotteness.
Twenty-four years like that, not even knowing
what had been taken. And then she was forgotten.
Let us remember poor Theroigne de Mericourt
who had ideas just ahead of her time
always remember to watch for your sisters
love them, but still keep the wall to your back.

Selected Poems

A Ballad of Abuse and Revenge

Crewcut and tonsured, hands like greedy steaks,
face carved of granite in a constant frown,
he seized our trouser belts and pulled them down
each time. 'I flog when anybody breaks

these very few and very simple rules.'
The leather strap was long as his long arm.
He told us flogging would not do us harm
and it was standard in the best of schools.

A textbook stolen. The wrong pair of shoes
worn in a classroom. Or scribbled slant
handwriting should be straight. I really can't
remember all his rules. He'd sometimes choose

one to be flogged for all. Sometimes my friend
slightly less camp than me. And sometimes me.
Peter and I discussed this over tea,
decided all this nonsense had to end.

It fucking hurt. We looked round then said fuck,
we felt quite guilty swearing. We were twelve
A few months less. You can't defend yourself
at that age. You are really out of luck.

We thought we'd change things. Maybe we could
    kill
headmaster Kevin. No one would believe
two smart queer kids could possibly conceive
that plan. We had no strength so brains and skill,

and watching waiting planning. When he drove
his battered car, he'd scrape along a wall.
What would it take, we thought, to make it fall?
Smiled at each other. Whipping marks fade mauve

then to pale lines. So Monte Cristo's count
became our model. Each and every day
stand by the wall each break and pull away
a little crumbled mortar. No amount

we couldn't scatter walking back to class.
He flogged us still. He also had his pets.
Athletes and jocks. A twelve year old forgets
so much. I know he never touched my arse

except with leather. But I felt his hate
felt flicks of sweat each time the strap would burn.
We listened every time he would return.
He took his favourites running. Came back late.

Worry they might get hurt? Not very much
They were his favourites so they took his cue
He picked on us. So they picked on us too
We smirked and guessed each of them felt his touch

along a thigh. We picked at mortar talked
of books and art and music. We'd compete
smart brainy kids also a bit effete
Started to guess ourselves as what we balked

at quite acknowledging. Our whole careers
started from those long talks. His intellect
my wit. His urge to win, mine to collect
great stacks of fact. Accepted we were queers.

And did not care. Murder was such a sin
we knew that we were damned would go to Hell
just hoped we'd drag him down with us as well.
Anger and pride – damnations all begin

with such. Our catechisms said our souls
were damned by bad intentions carried through
we shrugged and wept a bit as children do.
We picked at cracks and these became small holes.

The end was sudden. In a maths exam
heads down we scribbled and we heard a bang.
We thought if we were caught we'd hang.
He staggered past the window. We thought Damn!

His robes were tatters and the car a wreck
Our faces were the one thing that were straight
And eaten very cold revenge is great
Although we failed to break his fucking neck.

Many years later, when the scandal broke
after his death, a classmate.an MP,
had no idea, or so he said to me,
'I thought he always seemed a decent bloke.'

Roz Kaveney

A scribe of the house of the dead

1\. The calluses from holding his sharp pen
Stopped hurting him when he was nearly six.
He lost count of the symbols, had his tricks
To memorise then. His hands hurt again

when he was taught to draw and paint the gods
now he was worthy. One day he was whipped
he drew a face three-quarters on, full-lipped –
that time with flails, the second time with rods

and never broke their rules again. Instead
he dreamed the faces that he'd like to draw
and private symbols to express much more
than his stern masters knew was in his head

and by the time that he was twenty-one
had thought so much, he'd only just begun

2\. This much he knew – the sound, the word, the thing
The shape you draw, the thing the shape shows; all
Are cousins not the same, and yet you call
Them all the same. A simple copper ring

Both is and is not the great ring of gold
on Pharoah's finger. What they signify
is linked as his links Pharoah to the sky,
the Nile the land; yours to the wife you hold.

Selected Poems

And thus he came to know that nothing's real
as we conceive it, when we die we go
into some mystery we cannot know
until we step through death and start to feel

new air the things we know are symbols of.
He drew his scrolls with passionate new love.

3. He never talked about the things he thought,
distrusted words to hold them straight and true
nor painted them. A certain shade of blue
perhaps, it seemed to him, had almost caught

the thing he meant. He hoped it would convey
that thing to those who saw it; could not buy
or mix that pigment twice, and so let die
his hope. Aware that should his words betray

those thoughts, he'd die for heresy, but worse
the things the gods are symbols of would know
that he had failed them. It was best to go
quite silent through the world. There is a curse

that falls on thinkers who both fail in tact
and preach as truth that which is inexact.

4. And then he died, and found his death banal
exactly as he'd painted it for years.
He walked from mound to mound, and shed no
    tears

of fright as he fought snakes and lions, all

the creatures he had thought of as the mask
over some greater truth. His heart was weighed.
Anubis thanked him for his work. He prayed
For some enlightenment, but found no task

of learning strange new wisdom came to hand.
Gods talked to him, but told him nothing new
and, when he asked, said he had naught to do
for ever but be happy, kind and bland.

He spent eternity in discontent
Wondering what this was meant to represent.

Selected Poems

Book of the Dead

Game pieces on a board taught her the rules,
that she would really have to learn to read
and memorise the symbols that would lead
her to the Western Lands. All sorts of fools

might put their trust in someone else's spells,
bought with their names filled in, not understood
and they would end up drowning in their blood
or burned with fire. The Lord Anubis tells

those who are good from those who try to trick
the scales. There's one sits near him who devours
and as he bites the seconds seem like hours
of torture, fever, headache, being sick.

She prayed, and wrote, and drew to find the art
to make Death's feather balance with her heart.

She planned it all, had the best spices bought
and laid aside; on linen wrote down prayers
to wrap her in. She set all her affairs
in order, had her serving girls all taught

which priest to bring to open up her eyes
and mouth with virgin tools, which priest to cut
her organs neatly out, and gently put
them in gold jars, each of a different size,

heart, liver and the pieces of her brain.
The drying, and the bandages, and mask
of gold and lapis. Each maid had a task
and started on it when she felt the pain

of dying and snapped orders. Her last breath
words of control, of their lives and her death.

She lay dead in her tomb. After a while
she thought to rise, and leave her corpse behind,
dried, cold, perfected. She had hoped to find
little clay servants round her. She said 'I'll

go seek them out' then realised they were dust
around her coffin, but did not despair,
walked through the tomb wall into crisp cold air
under no sky. She felt both fear and trust

fear of the lands she'd walk, desert and marsh,
where crocodiles and lions lay in wait.
Her prayers and spells would turn away their hate,
Lead to Anubis' court, both fair and harsh.

She trusted that his judgement of her deeds
would bless her, lead her to the Land of Reeds.

The delta but no sea, streams, rivulets
the river flowing somewhere out of sight.
Small birds to catch or sing. Bright stars at night.
Warm but not burning sun. She soon forgets

her life in joy. Chasing red flowers that blow
upon light winds. Salt olives and sweet dates.
Tiny salt fish arranged on silver plates
to come across when hungry. And to go

with soothing rustling through the endless reeds.
And not to hear her bones and wrappings ground
in mortars, when apothecaries found
the medicine that every patient needs

that stinks and does no harm, nor hear a crowd
discuss her withered naked corpse aloud.

Roz Kaveney

Me Too

Soho was where I hung out with my friends
The seedy grubbiness of streets by day
Dust on cheap turned off neon tubes. The grey
Of unslept faces unbrushed hair split ends
Chipped varnish nails. There's something oddly real
When glamour's in its twentysecond hour
And fading but it still retains some power
For cynic aesthetes. Somehow it can steal
Upon you as it cannot in the night
All sequin and pretend that you belong
You've seen it lounge in a half torn sarong
It's not your home yet but one day it might
Let you. Dizzy on newly woman no control
Thinking I knew things I had yet to learn
Unschooled by pain. Still pretty. Green as fern
And fragile stagger innocent as foal
As thin longlegged and so he knew me prey
Managed three clubs and knew that I was trans
Six foot plus stylish boots and quite large hands
And was it seems his choice to fuck that day
A shoulder tap. A large suit seized my wrist
Aftershave muscles. Sudden through a door
I'd never noticed. Upstairs second floor
Office. Desk. Sofa. Photos. You could list
Celebrities he had upon his wall
Perhaps he knew. Walked over. Touched my hair
Stroked chin for stubble. Strutted to his chair
Black leather streaked in places. Trousers fall
Quite unselfconscious. And no underwear.

Knew what to do and did. Small soft and pink
And slightly bitter. Faster than you'd think
No threat except the large suit standing there
Watching and waiting. 'We've seen you around
Head in a book. We don't like our girls to read.
Want job? Don't need time off. You queens don't bleed.
Good workers. What I've nearly always found.
No?' pulled his trousers up and we were done
Face blank as paint. A tissue. Did my lips.
And left. Met Maz. Had shepherd's pie and chips
Took taste away. Soho no longer any fun
But just some streets. This pretty butch I knew
Seven years later crying over tea.
Turned out same guy same stuff the same as me
Sighed sisterguilt that I'd not warned. 'Me too.'

Recent Poems

Gaius Valerius' Will

Rome is not free. Its streets begin to chafe
My sides like sweat soiled linen. Head for home?
Sniff breeze off Garda? Wait for death in Rome.
Her brother died for him so she'll be safe.
Despising him was a mistake. Affairs,
Corruption do not matter as they should
The city's tired of boring clever good.
A laurel crown around his last few hairs
Throws coin. Is charming. Those few lines I wrote
Mocked him. And never changed a single mind.
Perfect last line, and one day soon I'll find
Rough men outside my door to cut my throat.
Beheading's quick if Caesar is not cruel.
Or slit veins. Dead before bath water's cool.

Selected Poems

The Mercy of Caesar

'Crosses the sea. Then Attis barefoot runs.'
A sword, a note, a clamp, a gelding knife
My lines. And so I end or change my life.
Did not expect my adolescent puns
About Mamurra's dick caused such offence.
Tyrants are witty. Does he know or guess
I've thought of this? I once put on her dress
In play. She fingered me. We got a sense
It went too far. She left me. It was hell.
I wept like Ariadne on the shore.
She'd laughed when I condemned her as a whore
Grave said you understand grief all too well.
Unmanly and unRoman. What's to lose?
Ounces of flesh that I despise. I choose.

Birdman by Frink – Pembroke College.

His glare with hollow eyes his killer jaw
Murderer bird and man long legged stalk
Mutter of blood and filth his only talk
Homicide predator tyrannosaur
Frink cast in bronze time eats all things but this
Will last a while and scare for years to come
Holding the memory of finger thumb
That moulded clay or wax before the kiss
Of burning metal. Fifty years ago
In a friend's room new bought when we were young
Years moulded burned us. Life's short art is long
They tell us always and we always know.
The brute beast creature time will kill devour
Make poems bronzes last beyond my hour.

Selected Poems

December 13th 2019

The unused gate hinge stiff flaked paint or rust
Path thick with bone break slush. Wind blows rain
    cold
Dim light at noon. Look for the graves that hold
Hope's loves. The headstones toppled. There's a crust
Of filth obscures each name. Whispering trees
Clutch finger branches darkling with regret
Fractal like years' despairs. Do not forget
What was was lost. Catch twist ache in your knees
That once could dance. Hate voice in ears would
    laugh
You'd try. Your own worst critic. You would fail
Slip ice slush polished floor. Rain turns to hail
Leave your cheap flowers. There's a steaming bath.
Deep under snow above the clouds and dark
Bulb green spears germinate, perhaps a lark.

Roz Kaveney

Abigail in Dream

She came to me, careworn as when she died
But not as pale. The pencil round her eyes
Dark sparkle laugh. It's never a surprise
The dead are quite laconic. I confide
My poems, loves, flirtations. She half-smiles.
I overshare a little. For ten years
I have not seen her. Joy. Regret. Some tears.
I beg her back in verse. As if there's miles
Between us or perhaps a thick glass wall
Words will not crack. Attempting to explain
Life since her death is losing her again
Orpheus failed. My songs don't work at all.
I wake. I think she warned me. But of what
She did not say or waking I forgot.

Lilith

She'd lain with him not made yet in the clay
And would not serve. Left Eden. Slammed the gate
Behind her with a clang. Sources debate
Her movements after that, She walked away
Unfallen proud, And mother. Screech owls fly
Her entourage. Briars tangle in her wake
Dark fruit stains lips and fingers for her sake
Loves wayward naughty children. It's a lie
She steals kills plagues. She rescues. To ignore
Refuse. She teaches. How to shed our skin
Avoid transcend. She whispers. We begin
As she taught sister lover Eve before.
Archangel seraph demon patriarch
Arouse then ride in velvet midnight dark.

Roz Kaveney

I slept so much

I slept so much those years. Woke thick with sleep
And bleary-eyed. Mascara spider tears
And gummy lashes. So much disappears
Whole weeks gone into dust that lies grey deep
On shelves that I can't reach don't know they're there
Friendships misfiled not even scrawled on card.
I do not have an index so it's hard
To know what's missing. Mostly I can't care.
Obituaries jog memories or in dream
They walk across the stage and wave. An ache
Where tooth was pulled. No point. I try to rake
My fingers through the dust. A shroud, no seam
Lies over things that I cannot unpick
Brain fog from anaesthesia so thick.

Selected Poems

For Larry Kramer

Survived a plague, died now. Still work undone.
Wrote to the end. Breath failed. And still his rage
Letters race wildfire char and light each page
Some prophets act like anger is their fun
His was Cassandra grief they did not hear.
More loved than liked. Distrust polite or nice.
He said things loud and louder said them twice
His was the powerlessness the great still fear
No limits. He would never compromise
Curmudgeon difficult embarrassment
Yet tender kind in passing. Garments rent
Sit mourning circle. When a great man dies
His flaws die. Saved lives. Wrote well. And his
    pride…
Be very glad that he was on our side.

Roz Kaveney

The Composers

Suspend a moment hovering in time
Kestrel or halcyon or butterfly
Give wood gut brass a voice that will not die
A universal tongue. I work with rhyme
Clattering dance of syllables in pairs
Quadrille at best. You all know where I go
A sudden turn a twist and sometimes slow
I pluck at grief. At best I rouse small hairs
Neck nape. Mystic arithmetic in rounds
Staring compassionate from higher peak
Parnassian. In vain we poets seek
Perfect from words what you achieve with sounds
Tease weep seduce enrage enchant entrance
We hear our mind caught reasoned into dance.

House in Jericho

I could not hear the screams. A haunted house
My housemate said. And shortly after packed
And left. I was aware – undoubted fact –
A room was missing. Once I saw a mouse
Come through a wall. And if I stood outside
There was a window on the second floor
That made no sense. I felt walls for a door
Painted or papered over. Once I tried
Looked from a ladder. But the room was dark
As space or midnight. Maybe wasn't there.
Levered the window standing on a chair
No purchase. Couldn't make a mark.
Mystery imagination maybe fear
Not sure what story I am telling here.

Roz Kaveney

Villonesque

I can't recall the last year that it snowed.
The white flakes falling from the sky are ash.
Once luscious lips now an unsmiling gash.
The murder van impatient in the road –
I lost some lottery or just grew old.
The women that I loved are mostly dead.
Forgotten is the last good book I read.
They process us for fat bone hair and gold.
The police are thugs have never been our friend
I laughed when someone hit one in the face
Perhaps quite soon a rock will fall from space
Our loves our yesterdays our snows will end.
Prince to whom loyalty would be a crime
Shit on your shoes, spit in your eyes this rhyme.

Selected Poems

For Grahame, Shepherd, Rackham and Vess

Small beasts that scurry in the undergrass
Or burrow lightly where the earth is turned
Or forage straws where stubble has been burned
Or quiet wait while plough and harrow pass
Then hustle to the safety of a hedge.
Small birds that heave long dried grass to their nest
Bees ants and mayflies. Grasshoppers. The rest
That buzz or whine among the leaves of sedge
That shelters moorhens, voles at edge of lake.
Frogs minnows slowworms harmless and afraid
Pink newborn creatures. Eggs this moment laid.
Breeze spell of shade and safety for their sake
The son of Hermes by Dryope born
He is the Piper at the Gates of Dawn.

Roz Kaveney

For Richard Dadd

There is a place where daisies grow like trees
Withered by a darkened sun whose dusky light
Stills air. The courtiers haughty but polite
Kirtles and pantaloons above their knees
Which bend at different angles. There's a sneer
Pervasive as a smell which fills the place
But never lingers long on any face
For epigram. They are assembled here
Witness a tardy sentence overdue
Old traitor bald as egg is in a trance
Smash him and then go somewhere else to dance
The woodman struck, was paid in fairy gold
Withered to leaves and teazels when he woke.
This was The Fairy Feller's Master Stroke.

Selected Poems

Gambit

It is the game. The rules. Black. White. Up Down.
Sixty-four squares. Black White. The fourteenth line
Where it all changes Their art is not mine.
Sometimes the least thing will attain the crown.
I move. The clock ticks on. The page. The board.
The final double beat that ends the game.
I have my favourite rhymes never the same.
Look back at how I play am sometimes awed
Not at myself. The forms. We're in the cave
And all is shadows. Something else is true
That we don't know but yet we struggle through
To something like. So poets misbehave
Players half mad. The rules. The forms. Black White.
I play myself quite late into the night.

Roz Kaveney

Memory of Don Giovanni

The statue comes but does not come to dine
He ate in Heaven. Does not need your food.
This is the only mercy of the good.
Be someone else you lecherous murderous swine.
Mozart, Da Ponte knew this very well.
Most freedom comes at somebody's expense
And pleasure's only in the present tense
And Don Giovanni is dragged off to Hell.
But he's the hero. Gets the best tunes. Free
To choose damnation as the cost of pride
The women he abuses mostly cried
Behind their fans masks veils. Annoyingly
That last ensemble does not quite persuade.
Ottavio gets the girl. Does not get laid.

Selected Poems

For Chip on his Birthday

I think of you as light, ripples on pool
Reflection fraction. Jewels on a string
Of glitter time. To grab the second thing
As well as what you chose. I walked from school
Bought all those early books I have them still
Like a tattoo shoulder-implanted cage
A songbird. Local cluster in a rage
Dynastic. It is not for love we kill
The ones we love but class or power or cash.
And ah! those bitten nails. We always find
New tricks with meaning to confound the mind.
Sometimes a kiss that bites. Sometimes a lash
Wounds the autumnal city. Fragments fall
Mosaic patterns that describe us all.

Roz Kaveney

Poems in a Time of Plague

LINES IN A TIME OF PLAGUE

Scribble on corner sofa champagne buzz
Sharp on my tongue the chatter in my ears
Echoes so many well-intentioned years
Of nice good people rooms. A full glass does
Remove a sense of doom. The night is cold
The wicked mean me harm. Quinoa canapés
Will not sustain me at the end of days.
I will not rant. I will not even scold.
Sweetness and moderation will console
For moments as will wine. We earn our fate
By pleasant vices we repent too late
That day by easy day corrode the soul.
Nothing but corpses strewn around the ball
Silence and the Red Death will conquer all.

I do not wish to leave. Out in the park
Squirrels play hide run up the winter trees
Rain still brings petrichor upon the breeze
Car splash light shatters wet roads in the dark.
Chocolate and ginger whisper hint my tongue
Some symphony's staccato trumpet line
Consoles sharp smooth a cello wind entwine
I listened more attentively when young
Fewer distractions and less work to do
To lose myself in making. There's a voice

Crisp in my mind that ratifies each choice
Each rhyme. And every night the touch of you.
Breath mingle. Heads on pillow gentle sigh
Awaken sleep dream laugh and never die.

Roz Kaveney

Poems in a Time of Plague

SCRIPTURE

No thing, or place, or time. Spark flickers dies.
Gone universe. It lasted all our years
comets fucks symphonies. Ended in tears.
That end. Or aren't. We're dust, but dust that lies

better than hopeless truth. Blood from a scratch
chili on tongue. A single perfect line.
Better than gods. One moment you were mine
Live die. To live is dying – that's the catch,

Contractual. Joy costs. These are the facts.
No gods but those we made up in our head
helped us to kill or love. They're just as dead.
We will not be remembered for our acts.

Stumble for meaning. If it's there, we're blind.
A second's light. Make art and love. Be kind.

Selected Poems

Poems in a Time of Plague

IN TIME OF PLAGUE

Simple. You whip the egg and grate the cheese
Chop basil melt some butter in the pan
Pour wait and fold. Warmed plate when you began
Buttered some bread and made a choice of teas.
Perhaps an apple. How we spend our days
Waiting for ends that may or may not come.
Something so small may summon with the thumb
It does not have. And meanwhile music plays
I change the disc Tchaikovsky and then Bach
And work a little. It is spring outside
Sun on my balcony. Last night I cried
For all we lose. Wrote an unkind remark
Thought better. Work. I must resist regret
For things done, things undone. There is time yet.

Roz Kaveney

For Shahin Shahablou

It was his art to see. Whose eyes are shut
In death. To share with everyone insight
Of how I looked to him. To catch the light
Shining behind me. Carefully would put
Me in an arch with endless trees behind
That were not infinite just look that way
In captured moment as the branches play
In wind – the day was cold. And he could find
Words that would make me smile and look my best
Forever. If my work lives that's my face
He took then gave me back to fix my place
In time. He's dead. I can't say he's at rest.
Choked slept the virus took away last breath
Curse fools and knaves betrayed him to his death

After Callimachus 22

The dawn was bright. The celebrants wore black.
Bore Melanippus in a slow cortege.
He should have not been dead at that young age.
Basilo, virgin sister, felt the lack
Of brother in her life. She could not bear
To go on breathing. Died by her own hand
At sunset that same day. To understand
Is pointless – all you have to do is share
Her sorrow. Saw her brother in the flame
And chose to follow. All Cyrene feels grief
Bowing our heads in pain without relief.
The last two heirs of such an honoured name
Are gone. Cut down by spiteful joyless fate.
Their house in darkness, empty, desolate.

Roz Kaveney

So many parties I did not enjoy
That much. Chase green light wait for great good time
Sometimes in moments that now stick like lime
In corners of a dream. Kissed girl or boy
Danced adequately. Made a bitch remark
Not quite regretted. Drank too much champagne
Ate canapés or crisps. Never again
Will we be as we were. My flat the park
The butcher, baker. Walking up and down
Six feet of balcony. I climb my stair
In salt taste exile. Panic thought at dare
See room of people. Never go to town.
Go masked in street. I will not show my tears
For things I did not know I loved those years

Selected Poems

Silent, and stunned asleep. Tubes in your veins
Tubes choke your throat to breathe to eat to drink
Bag round your arse to catch the constant stink
Of diarrhoea. Seven different pains
You do not know, yet feel though comatose
Balloon to keep your catheter in place.
The nurse comes by pats ice against your face
Sometimes you snort some fluid from your nose
The only sound you'll make until you die.
Perhaps you'll live. Your limbs will waste away.
Your lungs will rattle. And your tongue is grey
With scurf. Skin dust clogged in either eye.
Your world reduced, six inches of scrubbed floor.
You are your nation's perfect metaphor.

Roz Kaveney

The grief friends feel for friends we never met
Cannot be shared. Our words of comfort dumb.
They weep their mourning. Our tears must not come
Would be intrusion. Our task is to get
The cups of tea the glass of single malt,
Answer the phone say they will call back soon
Draw early blinds on summer afternoon
And disagree say it was not their fault.
Perhaps it was. A bit. We do not know
So cannot lie. Our job is to be kind
Care for their cares and disperturb their mind.
Change film or music. Keep the volume low.
Nor hope to comfort though we may assume
We help let comfort slowly join the room.

Also available from Team Angelica Publishing

Prose

'Reasons to Live' by Rikki Beadle-Blair
'What I Learned Today' by Rikki Beadle-Blair
'Faggamuffin' by John R Gordon
'Colour Scheme' by John R Gordon
'Souljah' by John R Gordon
'Drapetomania' by John R Gordon
'Hark' by John R Gordon
'Fairytales for Lost Children' by Diriye Osman
'Cuentos Para Niños Perdidos' – Spanish language edition of 'Fairytales', trans. Héctor F. Santiago
'Black & Gay in the UK' ed. John R Gordon & Rikki Beadle-Blair
'Sista! – an anthology' ed. Phyll Opoku-Gyimah, John R Gordon & Rikki Beadle-Blair
'More Than – the Person Behind the Label' ed. Gemma Van Praagh
'Tiny Pieces of Skull' by Roz Kaveney
'Fimí sílẹ̀ Forever' by Nnanna Ikpo
'Lives of Great Men' by Chike Frankie Edozien
'Lord of the Senses' by Vikram Kolmannskog

Playtexts

'Slap' by Alexis Gregory
'Custody' by Tom Wainwright
'#Hashtag Lightie' by Lynette Linton
'Summer in London' by Rikki Beadle-Blair
'I AM [NOT] KANYE WEST' by Natasha Brown

Poetry

'Charred' by Andreena Leeanne
'Saturn Returns' by Sonny Nwachukwu

www.ingramcontent.com/pod-product-compliance
Lightning Source LLC
LaVergne TN
LVHW051553080426
835510LV00020B/2963